The 1996 McGraw-Hill
Team and Organization
Development Sourcebook

The 1996 McGraw-Hill Team and Organization Development Sourcebook

Mel Silberman

Assisted by
Carol Auerbach

McGraw-Hill

New York San Francisco Washington, D.C. Auckland Bogotá
Caracas Lisbon London Madrid Mexico City Milan
Montreal New Delhi San Juan Singapore
Sydney Tokyo Toronto

International Standard Serial Number:
The 1996 McGraw-Hill Team and Organization Development Sourcebook
ISSN 1084-1350

Copyright © 1996 by The McGraw-Hill Companies, Inc. All rights reserved. Printed in the United States of America. Except as permitted under the United States Copyright Act of 1976, no part of this publication may be reproduced or distributed in any form or by any means, or stored in a database or retrieval system, without the prior written permission of the publisher.

Although this publication remains subject to copyright, permission is granted free of charge to make up to 100 photocopies per year of the forms which are required by participants attending a training session. This permission does not apply to material reprinted in this book for which permission must be obtained from the original copyright holder. Photocopying may be performed by the individual purchaser only. Under no circumstances will any reproduction of the designated materials or any portion thereof be either sold or distributed on a commercial basis without the permission of McGraw-Hill. Except as expressly provided above, no part of this book may be reproduced or distributed in any form or by any means, or stored in a database or retrieval system, without the prior written permission of McGraw-Hill. For permission to reprint more than 100 copies per year, please call Mary Johnson, (212) 512-2574, McGraw-Hill Permissions Department.

1 2 3 4 5 6 7 8 9 0   EDW/EDW   9 0 0 9 8 7 6 5   (Paperback)
1 2 3 4 5 6 7 8 9 0   EDW/EDW   9 0 0 9 8 7 6 5   (Looseleaf)

ISBN 0-07-057673-4 (Paperback)
ISBN 0-07-057674-2 (Looseleaf)

The sponsoring editor for this book was Richard Narramore, the editing supervisor was Fred Dahl, the designer was Inkwell Publishing Services, and the production supervisor was Pamela Pelton.

Printed and bound by Edwards Brothers.

McGraw-Hill books are available at special quantity discounts to use as premiums and sales promotions, or for use in corporate training programs. For more information, please write to the Director of Special Sales, McGraw-Hill, 11 West 19th Street, New York, NY 10011. Or contact your local bookstore.

Are you interested in being a contributor to *The 1997 McGraw-Hill Team and Organization Development Sourcebook?*

In the course of your professional work, you have probably developed exercises, handouts, instruments, short articles, and other printed materials that could be useful to a wide audience of consultants, trainers, and team leaders. Consider your favorite piece of work for publication. The *1997 Sourcebook* will contain another 40 practical tools to improve team and organizational effectiveness. Would you like to contribute one of them?

For more information, contact:

Mel Silberman, Editor
The McGraw-Hill Team and Organization Development Sourcebook
c/o Active Training
26 Linden Lane
Princeton, NJ 08540
609-924-8157
609-924-4250 fax
mel@tigger.jvnc.net

CONTENTS

ASSESSMENT INSTRUMENTS 81

HELPFUL HANDOUTS   123

PRACTICAL GUIDES   157

TOPICAL INDEX
Find a Tool for Your Specific Topic

In the place of a traditional index is the following classification by topic of the 40 tools found in *The 1996 McGraw-Hill Team and Organization Development Sourcebook.*

PREFACE

Welcome to the inaugural edition of *The McGraw-Hill Team and Organization Development Sourcebook,* a yearly collection of practical tools to develop team and organizational effectiveness.

Along with its companion, *The McGraw-Hill Training and Performance Sourcebook, The McGraw-Hill Team and Organization Development Sourcebook* provides the latest cutting-edge advice and learning aids on topics important to today's public and private sector organizations. While *The Training and Performance Sourcebook* emphasizes development and support at the individual level of the organization, *The McGraw-Hill Team and Organization Development Sourcebook* focuses on organizationwide issues.

Having *The McGraw-Hill Team and Organization Development Sourcebook* available for instant reference allows you to select printed materials on team and organizational change written by leading experts. In addition, the *Sourcebook* serves as a state-of-the-art clearinghouse of ideas and new practices. It helps you keep up with the spiraling developments in the field of team and organization development.

The 1996 Sourcebook contains 40 team activities, assessment instruments, handouts, and practical guides—creating a ready-to-use toolkit for consultants, trainers, and team leaders. It is also invaluable for team sponsors, managers, and other organizational representatives who are interested in team and organization development. Best of all, because these tools are reproducible, they can be shared with others.

Here are some of the topics covered in *The 1996 McGraw-Hill Team and Organization Development Sourcebook:*

✓ Assessment of team functioning
✓ Conflict resolution
✓ Cooperation and trust building
✓ Creative problem solving
✓ Customer service
✓ Goal setting and planning
✓ Facilitating teams
✓ Managing and leading change
✓ Organizational initiatives

✓ Quality and continuous improvement

✓ Team development

I hope you will find *The 1996 McGraw-Hill Team and Organization Development Sourcebook* to be a one-stop resource you can draw on again and again in your efforts to facilitate team and organizational effectiveness.

Mel Silberman
Princeton, New Jersey

The 1996 McGraw-Hill
Team and Organization
Development Sourcebook

TEAM ACTIVITIES

In this section of *The 1996 McGraw-Hill Team and Organization Development Sourcebook,* you will find sixteen team activities. They are designed to:

✓ Sell teamwork and cooperation.

✓ Set goals.

✓ Establish team trust.

✓ Build cohesion.

✓ Develop problem-solving skills.

✓ Increase information flow.

✓ Resolve conflicts.

You can use these activities in a variety of settings:

✓ Team-building sessions

✓ Meetings

✓ Retreats

✓ Training programs

✓ Consultations

All the activities featured here are highly participatory. They are designed with the belief that learning and change best occur through *experience* and *reflection.* As opposed to preaching or lecturing, experiential activities place people directly in a concrete situation. Typically, participants are asked to solve a problem, complete an assignment, or communicate information. Often the task can be quite challenging. Sometimes, it can also be a great deal of fun. The bottom line, however, is that participants become active partners in learning new concepts or in developing new ideas.

The experiences contained in the activities you are about to read can also be of two kinds: *simulated* and *real-world.* Although some may find them to be artificial, well designed simulations can provide an effective analogy to real-world experiences. They also have the advantage of being time-saving shortcuts to longer, drawn-out activities. Sometimes, of course, there is no substitute for real-world experience. Activities that engage teams in actual, ongoing work can serve as a powerful mechanism for change.

Experience, by itself, is not always "the best teacher." Reflecting on the experience, however, can yield wisdom and insight. You will find that the team activities in this section contain helpful guidelines for reflection. Expect a generous selection of questions to process or debrief the actual activities.

All the activities here have been written for ease of use. A concise overview of each activity is provided. You will be guided, step-by-step, through the activity instructions. All the necessary participant materials are included. For your photocopying convenience, these materials are on separate pages. Any materials you need to prepare in advance have been kept to a minimum. Special equipment or physical arrangements are seldom needed.

Best of all, the activities are designed so that you can easily modify or customize them to your specific requirements. Also, time allocations are readily adaptable. Furthermore, many of the activities are "frame exercises"—generic activities that can be used for many topics or subject matter. You will find it easy to plug in the content relevant to your team's circumstances.

As you conduct any of these activities, bear in mind that experiential activity is especially successful if you do a good job as facilitator. Here are some common mistakes people make when facilitating experiential activities:

1. *Motivation:* Participants aren't invited to buy into the activity themselves or sold the benefits of joining in. Participants don't know what to expect during the exercise.

2. *Directions:* Instructions are lengthy and unclear. Participants cannot visualize what the facilitator expects from them.

3. *Group Process:* Subgroups are not composed effectively. Group formats are not changed to fit the requirements of each activity. Subgroups are left idle.

4. *Energy:* Activities move too slowly. Participants are sedentary. Activities are long or demanding when they need to be short or relaxed. Participants do not find the activity challenging.

5. *Processing:* Participants are confused and/or overwhelmed by the questions posed to them. There is a poor fit between the facilitator's questions and the goals of the activity. The facilitator shares his/her opinions before first hearing the participants' views.

To avoid these pitfalls, follow these steps:

I. Introduce the activity.

1. Explain your objectives.

2. Sell the benefits.

3. Convey enthusiasm.

4. Connect the activity to previous activities.

5. Share personal feelings and express confidence in participants.

II. Help participants know what they are expected to do.
   1. Speak slowly.
   2. Use visual backup.
   3. Define important terms.
   4. Demonstrate the activity.

III. Manage the group process.
   1. Form groups in a variety of ways.
   2. Vary the number of people in any activity based upon that exercise's specific requirements.
   3. Divide participants into teams before giving further directions.
   4. Give instructions separately to groups in a multipart activity.
   5. Keep people busy.
   6. Inform the subgroups about time frames.

IV. Keep participants involved.
   1. Keep the activity moving.
   2. Challenge the participants.
   3. Reinforce participants for their involvement in the activity.
   4. Build physical movement into the activity.

V. Get participants to reflect on the activity's implications.
   1. Ask relevant questions.
   2. Carefully structure the first processing experiences.
   3. Observe how participants are reacting to the group processing.
   4. Assist a subgroup that is having trouble processing an activity.
   5. Hold your own reactions until after hearing from participants.

FORMING, STORMING, NORMING, AND PERFORMING: A CARD SORT EXERCISE

Tim Osgood

Tim Osgood *is program manager, Market Development Group, in Du Pont External Affairs (BMP16-2110, PO Box 80016, Wilmington, DE 19880, 302-992-6150). He consults with senior managers and global business team leaders on strategic thinking processes. His current interest is the development of innovative approaches to increase the capacity of individuals and teams to lead and manage the systemic changes required to revitalize competitive business performance. Tim is a doctoral candidate in the Psychoeducational Processes Program at Temple University.*

Overview This activity is an active, team-based strategy to learn about the four stages of team development that Tuckman* has labeled: *forming, storming, norming,* and *performing.* Instead of listening to someone lecture about the topic, participants are asked to classify events that occur in teams according to stage. By sorting cards that list these events, they learn about the different stages.

Suggested Time 30 minutes

Materials Needed
- ✓ Form A (Stages of Team Development)
- ✓ Form B (Events That Occur in Teams)
- ✓ Form C (Answers to Card Sort Exercise)
- ✓ Form D (Events Occurring at Different Stages)
- ✓ Decks of cards corresponding to the number of teams that you have.

Procedure
1. Tell the participants that this exercise will give them the opportunity to learn about the stages of team development in an active way.

2. Distribute Form A and ask participants to read it to themselves. Hold a brief discussion on the essential character of each stage.

*B. Tuckman (1965). Developmental Sequence in Small Groups, *Psychological Bulletin,* 63, 384–399.

3. Divide the total group into teams of four to eight members or conduct the exercise with one or more intact teams.

4. Distribute to each team a set of 24 index cards that each contains one of the 24 statements listed on Form B. Place the number corresponding to each statement in the upper-right corner of each card. For example, the first card in each set will look like this:

```
                                                          1



Members are concerned with
acceptance.
```

5. Explain that there are 24 cards in each set. Exactly 6 cards contain statements referring to each of the four stages: *forming, storming, norming,* and *performing*. Inform teams that they have 15 minutes to sort the cards into four piles corresponding to the stages.

6. Call time and distribute Form C to each team. Ask each team to obtain a score corresponding to the number of cards correctly classified. (If there is more than one team doing the exercise, declare the team with the highest score the winner.)

7. Distribute Form D. Ask each team to study the correct answers.

8. Reconvene the total group and discuss the significance of the answers. If the teams participating in the exercise are actual work teams, invite them to assess the apparent stage of team development for their teams. Ask each team to explain the reasoning for its assessment.

Forming: Transition stage, characterized by movement from individual to team member status. This is a period of confusion, testing behavior, and dependence on a team leader for direction.

Storming: Conflict stage, characterized by infighting, defensiveness, and competition. Team members respond emotionally to and resist task demands.

Norming: Cohesion stage, characterized by an acceptance of team norms and roles. Team members work to achieve harmony.

Performing: Work stage, characterized by maximum work accomplishment, high-level problem solving and decision making, as well as personal insight and constructive self-change.

1. Members are concerned with acceptance.
2. Delegation is the prevailing leadership style.
3. The team communicates openly.
4. Conflict continues to occur.
5. Goals are not clear, but clarity is not sought.
6. The team encourages innovation.
7. Cohesion and trust increase.
8. Members communicate in a tentative manner.
9. Clarification of goals begins.
10. Participation increases.
11. Member satisfaction increases.
12. Conflicts about values surface.
13. The team leader is seen as benevolent and competent.
14. Subgroups and coalitions form.
15. The team leader's role becomes more consultative.
16. Subgroups work on important tasks.
17. The team assumes that consensus about goals exists.
18. Subgroups and coalitions are rare.
19. Goal clarity and consensus increase.
20. Pressures to conform increase.
21. Dissent is tolerated.
22. Role clarification begins.
23. The team has defined its work.
24. Decreased conformity begins.

Forming	*Total Obtained*
1 5 8 13 17 18	

Storming	*Total Obtained*
9 10 12 14 22 24	

Norming	*Total Obtained*
4 7 11 15 19 20	

Performing	*Total Obtained*
2 3 6 16 21 23	

Team Score

EVENTS OCCURRING AT DIFFERENT STAGES*

Forming

Members are concerned with acceptance.

Goals are not clear but clarity is not sought.

Members communicate in a tentative manner.

The team leader is seen as benevolent and competent.

The team assumes that consensus about goals exists.

Subgroups and coalitions are rare.

Storming

Clarification of goals begins.

Participation increases.

Conflicts about values surface.

Subgroups and coalitions form.

Role clarification begins.

Decreased conformity begins.

Norming

Conflict continues to occur.

Cohesion and trust increase.

Member satisfaction increases.

The team leader's role becomes more consultative.

Goal clarity and consensus increase.

Pressures to conform increase.

Performing

Delegation is the prevailing leadership style.

The team communicates openly.

The team encourages innovation.

Subgroups work on important tasks.

Dissent is tolerated.

The team has defined its work.

*Based on Susan A. Wheelan, *Group Processes: A Developmental Perspective,* Needham Heights, MA: Allyn & Bacon, 1994.

FIRST TOUCH:
A NEGOTIATION EXERCISE

Sivasailam Thiagarajan

As president of Workshops by Thiagi (4423 East Trailridge, Bloomington, IN 47408, 812-332-1478), **Sivasailam (Thiagi) Thiagarajan,** *Ph.D., specializes in designing and delivering training for improving human performance. Thiagi has been the president of the National Society for Performance and Instruction (NSPI) and of the North American Simulation and Gaming Association (NASAGA). He is the author of 24 books, more than 175 articles, and several hundred games and simulations.*

Overview Most people have heard about—and accepted—the concept of win–win solutions. But it is amazing how easily we all slip into a win–lose mode. This simple design requires only a few minutes to demonstrate how people prevent themselves from discovering and implementing win–win solutions. The implications for teams and organizations can be profound.

Suggested Time 10 minutes

Materials Needed *First Touch* cards, one copy for each triad.
(Photocopy Form A to produce these cards.)

Procedure 1. Ask the participants to organize themselves into trios. Appoint one person in each trio to be the card holder and give him or her a *First Touch* card.

2. Tell participants that the game is very simple and the rule for winning (and losing) is printed on the card. Explain that the card holder has two responsibilities:

✓ To hold the card firmly with the printed side up, parallel to the floor

✓ To silently observe the behavior of the two players

3. After the card holder holds the card according to your instructions, ask the other two players to extend their right index fingers and hold them approximately 6 inches above the surface of the card, pointing to the card.

4. Ask the players to read the rules on the card. Repeat the rules:

   ✓ You win if you get the other player to touch this card first.

   ✓ You lose if you touch the card first.

   Explain that the players can use any strategy they want to.

5. Walk among the different trios and observe what the players are doing. Make a mental note of different strategies.

6. After about 2 minutes or whenever the majority of players have concluded the game, stop the play. Here are some suggested questions to debrief the players:

   ✓ How many of you won? How do you feel about winning?

   ✓ How many of you lost? How do you feel about losing?

   ✓ If both players had touched the card at the same time, they both would have won. Do you agree?

   ✓ Most people immediately assume that if one person is to win, the other should lose. Do you agree?

   ✓ The presence of an observer usually increases the intensity of competition between the two players. Do you agree?

   ✓ The presence of other triads increases the intensity of competition. Do you agree?

   ✓ What real-world situations does this game reflect?

   ✓ What would have happened if the winners received a cash prize?

   ✓ What would have happened if two players agreed to touch the card simultaneously and one cheated at the last moment?

   ✓ If we played the same game again, how would you behave differently?

   ✓ How would you change the way you behave in similar situations in the real world?

You WIN
if you get
the other player
to touch
this card
first.

You LOSE
if you touch
this card
first.

WORLD HUNGER: TEAM COLLABORATION OR COMPETITION?

Jeffrey Backal and Merrick Rosenberg

Jeffrey Backal and Merrick Rosenberg are partners at Team Builders Plus (1873 Route 70 East, Suite 302, Cherry Hill, NJ 08003, 609-596-4196), an experience-based development firm specializing in creating productive and supportive work environments that get results through people. Selected clients include AAA, Air Products & Chemicals, Anderson Consulting, Coopers & Lybrand, Discover Card, Hewlett–Packard, ICI America, MBNA America, SmithKline Beecham, and Union Fidelity Life Insurance. Jeff and Merrick each have 10 years of experience in team building, leadership development, organizational development, and change management. Together they have designed many widely used experiential activities.

Overview This activity helps participants to understand and overcome the barriers to effective teamwork. It should be conducted with 10 to 40 participants. The group is divided in half and set up as if they were two competing teams trying to *win*. Ultimately, participants realize that they are on the same team and must work together to reach their common goal. The activity parallels many organizational issues, such as competition between departments, the benefits of working toward common goals, and the importance of effective communication.

Suggested Time 15–30 minutes

Materials Needed
✓ Form A (Group A Instructions)
✓ Form B (Group B Instructions)
✓ Four 20-foot pieces of rope or masking tape (used to make a 20-foot by 20-foot square border)
✓ 25 Toy spiders and snakes (paper plates used as "land mines placed by natives" can be substituted)
✓ 15 Bandannas

Procedure 1. Prior to participants entering the room, construct a 20-foot by 20-foot square on the ground using the four pieces of rope or tape.

2. Randomly place bandannas, spiders, and snakes (or paper plates) inside the square.

3. Divide the group in half, placing the two groups directly across from each other on the outside of the square playing field. Explain that the area contained within the ropes is *Sulfur Valley*.

4. Give Form A to one group and Form B to the other group. Instruct the groups to read their instructions quietly. Tell them that they may enter Sulfur Valley when they are ready. (To foster competition, you may want to print Forms A and B on different colored paper. Also, while the groups are reading their directions, you can subtly prompt them to enter the valley as quickly as possible by quietly saying to each group, "The other group seems about ready to enter the valley. You may want to start retrieving bandannas.")

5. Watch the participants in Sulfur Valley to make sure that they keep their eyes closed and do not step on any of the obstacles (that is, snake or spider). If a participant steps on an obstacle in the valley, he or she must relinquish all bandannas that he or she is holding (by dropping them in the field of play) and they must exit the valley. (They may reenter the valley.)

6. In most instances, neither group will gather the 10 required bandannas (for example, one group will retrieve seven bandannas, while the other group gathers eight). You can either end the activity at this point or you can say, "Tell me when you are done." The latter approach gives participants the opportunity to realize that if both groups combine their bandannas they will solve world hunger. This method allows them to feel both the negative effects of competition and the positive benefits of cooperation.

7. Key processing points:
   ✓ Did you think win–lose or win–win?
   ✓ Did the two groups work together?
   ✓ What assumptions were made? Why?
   ✓ Did you have a common goal? Did you work together toward that goal?
   ✓ How was communication? Was it difficult to hear instructions while you were in the valley? Why?
   ✓ What could have been done to improve communication?
   ✓ Was there a leader?
   ✓ Was there a plan?
   ✓ How did trust play into this activity?
   ✓ How does this replicate the workplace?

Your group has been on a long and dangerous journey to seek the cure for world hunger. Tens of thousands of people are dying each day from starvation and, without the cure, humans will soon become an endangered species.

You have wandered the forests of Kazmania for over 5 months. Your ration of nontoxic water is in short supply. You have barely enough food to last your group through the week. Your quest to date has been unsuccessful, but you have just discovered an ancient tablet in the outskirts of the Wala Wala village. The tablet contains the clue needed to complete your mission and it reads:

Ten bandannas are world hunger's clues
Step on a creature and you lose
Sulfur Valley emits gas that blinds
But it only lasts within its lines.

The bandannas contained in the valley represent the secrets. Unfortunately, Sulfur Valley emits a sulfur gas that causes blindness to individuals while they are in the valley. It is in your best interest to avoid all other objects in the valley as they are known to cause injury to those who touch them.

Rules and Objectives (for those who need to have rules clearly stated):

- ✓ Eyes must remain closed while in Sulfur Valley.
- ✓ Avoid all objects in the valley, or else.
- ✓ Collect ten bandannas and you have solved the cure for world hunger.

HAVE A SAFE AND PRODUCTIVE JOURNEY

Your group has been on a long and dangerous journey to seek the cure for world hunger. Tens of thousands of people are dying each day from starvation and, without the cure, humans will soon become an endangered species.

You have wandered the forests of Kazmania for over 5 months. Your ration of nontoxic water is in short supply. You have barely enough food to last your group through the week. Your quest to date has been unsuccessful, but you have just discovered an ancient tablet in the outskirts of the Wala Wala village. The tablet contains the clue needed to complete your mission and it reads:

Ten bandannas are world hunger's clues
Step on a creature and you lose
Sulfur Valley emits gas that blinds
But it only lasts within its lines.

The bandannas contained in the valley represent the secrets. Unfortunately, Sulfur Valley emits a sulfur gas that causes blindness to individuals while they are in the valley. It is in your best interest to avoid all other objects in the valley as they are known to cause injury to those who touch them.

Rules and Objectives (for those who need to have rules clearly stated):

    ✓ Eyes must remain closed while in Sulfur Valley.

    ✓ Avoid all objects in the valley, or else.

    ✓ Collect ten bandannas and you have solved the cure for world hunger.

HAVE A SAFE AND PRODUCTIVE JOURNEY

THE CHALLENGES AHEAD: A TEAM SELF-ASSESSMENT EXERCISE

Robert Barner

Robert Barner *is vice president of Parry Consulting Services (Suite 207, Plaza 222, U.S. Highway 1, Tequesta, FL 33469-2708, 407-747-1762), an international training and consulting service. Bob is also a well-known public speaker and writer. He is the author of* **Crossing the Minefields: Tactics for Overcoming Today's Toughest Management Challenges** *(AMACOM, 1994) and* **Lifeboat Strategies: How to Keep Your Career above Water during Tough Times … or Any Time** *(AMACOM, 1993).*

Overview   This exercise is designed to help teams evaluate their preparedness for meeting emerging performance challenges. It is particularly useful when facilitating teams that are:

✓ Operating within a high-change work environment.

✓ Attempting to meet changing customer requirements.

✓ Determining the most effective way of focusing their work efforts.

✓ Evaluating options for changing their structure or membership.

Suggested Time   90 minutes

Materials Needed
✓ Flip chart, color markers
✓ Form A (External Challenges and Opportunities)
✓ Form B (Internal Changes)
✓ Form C (The Impact–Preparedness Grid)
✓ View graph of Form C
✓ Overhead projector and screen

Procedure
1. Explain that team members typically have uniquely different views of the challenges and opportunities facing their team. This exercise enables participants to blend these views into a composite picture that can help the team establish clear future direction.

2. Inform team members that they will be asked to identify potential challenges and opportunities facing their team. To help "prime the pump" for ideas, take 5 minutes to review Form A, which provides examples of representative external challenges and opportunities facing hypothetical teams.

3. Give members 5 minutes to *individually* list, on a blank sheet of paper, several external challenges and opportunities that they feel that their team may soon be encountering.

4. Write the words *External Challenges and Opportunities* on the top of a piece of flip chart paper. Create a right-hand column with the header I for impact and P for preparedness.

External Challenges and Opportunities	*I*	*P*

5. Take 10 minutes to record team members' suggestions regarding perceived external challenges and opportunities. List all perceived changes. Allow no discussion on these changes until all are listed. Ignore the I and P columns for now. You will return to them later.

6. Explain that the next step enables team members to identify changes that are likely to occur *within the team* that could affect the team's ability to effectively respond to new challenges and opportunities.

7. To help "prime the pump" for ideas, take 5 minutes to review Form B, which provides examples of representative internal changes facing hypothetical teams.

8. Give members 5 minutes to *individually* record on another blank sheet of paper potential internal changes that their team may soon be facing.

9. Write the word *Internal Changes* on another flip chart sheet. Then take 10 minutes to record team members' suggestions regarding perceived internal changes. Once again, list all perceived changes and allow no discussion on these changes until all are listed. Post the flip chart for later review.

10. Explain that the next step allows team members to evaluate the relative importance of each of the external challenges and opportunities that they had earlier identified.

11. Using a 1 to 7 scale, with 7 representing greatest impact, take 10 minutes to have team members rate the likely *impact* of each change that they have listed. Average members' scores for each listing and record these averages in the appropriate I column of the *External Challenges and Opportunities* chart.

12. Next, using the same 1 to 7 scale, give participants an additional 10 minutes to plot their preparedness for dealing with each of the challenges and opportunities that they have listed. To do this, the team

should consider the overall affect of all the internal changes that they listed earlier. Average members' scores for each listing and record these averages in the appropriate P column of the *External Challenges and Opportunities* chart. Post the flip chart for later review. *Example:* Participants determine that they lack the technical skills needed to master a new, challenging work responsibility and that the one team member who is most competent to handle this new work responsibility will soon be transferred to a different department. As a result, they would probably give themselves a low preparedness score (1 to 3) for this challenge.

13. Explain that in the next step team members will be asked to assess their readiness for successfully addressing both the external challenges and opportunities and internal changes that they face. To do this, they will be asked to plot each event that they have identified thus far on the *Impact–Preparedness Grid* (Form C).

14. Prepare a transparency of the grid. Using a transparency marker, have the team take 5 minutes to plot each external challenge and opportunity on the grid. Use different letter abbreviations to represent each event. For example, the event "Extending our customer support services to new field offices" might be symbolized by the letters "FO" for field offices.

15. Take 5 minutes to explain the Impact–Preparedness Grid to participants, as follows:

    ✓ Events plotted in the Comfort Zone column are those that fall within the team's comfort zone; that is, they exert only a minimal impact on team performance (low impact) and participants feel that they are highly prepared to meet events. The team should spend the *least amount of time and effort* on managing these events.

    ✓ Events located in the Challenge Zones are those that represent a moderate level of challenge; the level of challenge (impact) that they represent is balanced by the team's level of preparedness. Give these events *a moderate level of attention*.

    ✓ Events located in the Danger Zone *deserve the team's greatest attention*, because these are the critical (high-impact) events that the team is least prepared to address. These are the events on which the team needs to focus.

16. If time permits, begin to develop actions plans for addressing these most critical challenges. Or suggest another meeting time to begin the process.

✓ A customer service team will soon be asked to provide assistance to new field offices, forcing them to stretch staff and coordinate efforts with new managers.

✓ An information systems team feels that it will be asked to provide less hands-on programming to one of its main internal customers, the engineering department. At the same time, it will be expected to play a larger consulting and advising role in helping the department to select appropriate software from outside vendors.

✓ A training team will soon be asked by their corporate office to provide make or buy comparisons showing how much it costs the company to use the team for a given service, as opposed to purchasing that service from outside vendors. The team feels that this change will put them under more pressure to justify their costs and operate in an efficient manner.

✓ A human resource team has been told that some of its services will soon be completely outsourced. The team will be responsible for selecting qualified vendors and maintaining the quality of these vendors.

✓ A purchasing team is being pressured to find ways to reduce the time it takes to complete purchase orders, forcing it to examine its work processes.

✓ As a result of a recent change in its senior management, a finance team may soon be asked to play a much bigger role in the development of its company's project proposals.

✓ A training team is being ask to expand its organizational role. Aside from providing training courses, it will soon be asked to provide departmental team-building programs and quality improvement seminars.

✓ A human resource team is under pressure by its departmental customers to become responsive and accessible. This means finding a way to put the human resource representatives more in touch with the day-to-day operations of the other departments.

✓ Two key people will soon be leaving on a finance team. The team feels that the loss of these members will weaken their overall bench strength.

✓ Several members of a quality assurance team are scheduled to complete in-depth training in implementation of quality improvement teams. These skills should place the team in a better position to address potential requests for these teams by other departments.

✓ A training team will soon be forced to split its staff in an effort to address the training needs of first- and second-shift employees.

✓ A media services team has just been approved for the purchase of a sophisticated software program that will enable the team to create in-house, computerized media programs now purchased by them from the outside.

✓ A service repair team will soon begin experimenting with a cross-training effort that should provide the team with more flexible coverage on service calls.

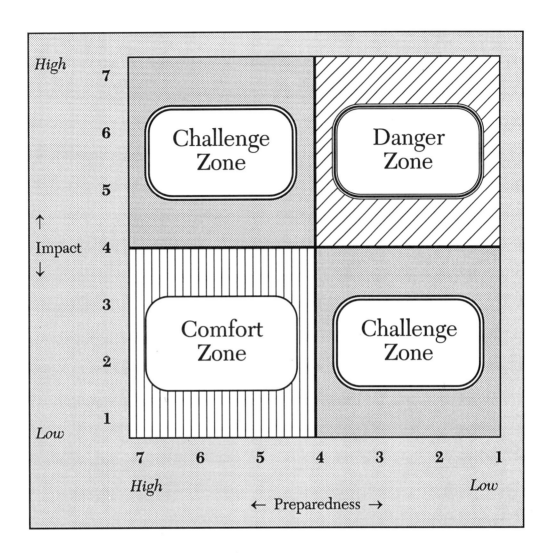

THE 20,000-VOLT WIRE: AN EXERCISE IN TRUST AND TEAMWORK

Bert Nemcik

Bert Nemcik, *Ph.D., is the training director for the Abraxas Foundation (Abraxas @vaxa.clarion.edu), an adolescent alcohol or drug rehabilitation program with 17 sites in Pennsylvania, West Virginia, and Ohio. He is the founder of the Lifelong Learning Network (RD 2, Marienville, PA 16239, 814-927-5640), a private consulting firm dedicated to advancing adult learning practices. He has published 15 electronic texts covering topics such as human motivation, supervision, and adult learning. He writes a weekly newspaper column entitled "Life, Liberty, and Library."*

Overview   This activity gives participants the opportunity to work physically and mentally to solve a team problem. Participants will learn to trust one another as they accomplish the task set before them. It is good way to begin a longer team-building process since it sets the stage for other activities that build on one another to develop a solid team. This activity will work with up to 20 participants. If there are more than 20, break the team into two smaller groups.

Suggested Time   40 minutes

Materials Needed   Large floor space, at least 15 feet wide; nylon string; masking tape; mats if the floor is not carpeted.

Procedure   1. Before the instructions are given, stretch the string across the room from wall to wall about 5 to 6 feet high. Tape the string to the wall. For safety reasons, do not tie it. Tell all participants to stand on one side of the string.

2. Tell the participants that this is a trust-building activity that will give them the opportunity to explore their level of trust with one another and assist them in breaking down any barriers that may exist within the team.

3. Explain to them what they are to do with the following words:

This is a 20,000-volt high-voltage wire. You cannot touch it or you will be electrocuted. Now, as a team, your mission, if you wish to accept it, is to pass each one of your team members over the wire and onto the other side. You cannot touch the wire. If you do, you must begin all over again. If you knock the wire down, you must start again. You cannot go under the wire. You must go over it. My only word of advice is to pass the largest individuals over first. You decide among yourselves how you want to accomplish this task. You can begin whenever you are ready.

4. Stand back and permit the team to begin. Ensure that the ground rules are adhered to and that the activity proceeds safely. If there is anything the team is doing that might be considered to be unsafe, intervene immediately.

5. After the team successfully completes the task, ask all the participants the following questions:

   a. What were some of your thoughts and feelings concerning trust as you were involved in this activity? What did you and others do to inspire trust? To diminish it?

   b. What did you notice about the communication process that was taking place as this activity started? As it proceeded? As you came close to getting the last person over? After the last person was over?

   c. What was helpful or not helpful about how you worked together?

   d. How did leadership emerge? Did any gender issues emerge?

   e. If you were going to undertake this activity all over again, what kinds of things would you do differently the second time?

   f. What are the most important things you can learn from this activity about yourself as a team member? As a team?

Variations:

1. As the participants are struggling to get over the hot wire, photograph them working with one another. Photographs can be shared with the team later as a graphic portrayal of their having worked hard to develop a strong, trusting team.

2. If the group is comprised of many physically unfit people, the string can be initially lowered to about 4 feet so that the team members can successfully complete the exercise.

3. If the group is comprised of many younger participants who are physically fit, then the string can be raised to 6 or 7 feet to make the activity challenging for them.

DELIVERING AN EGG UNBROKEN: A TEAM CHALLENGE

6

Ed Rose

Ed Rose, *training manager for Harris Semiconductor in Palm Bay, Florida, has over 30 years experience with teams and teamwork both in industry and the world of sports. He presents internationally on the subject of self-directed work teams and has published numerous articles and papers on self-directed work teams in technical journals and magazines. Ed played on five world championship softball teams. He can be reached at 5400 Sand Lake Drive, Melbourne, Florida 32934, 407-724-7560.*

Overview   In this activity, a team is challenged to accomplish a task within a time limit: to design a delivery system, as a team, that will protect a raw egg dropped from a height of 8 feet onto a hard surface. Production, design, presentation skills, and teamwork with these real-life time constraints all play a part in the challenge. This exercise is only limited by the mind of the facilitator. It has been used successfully as a warm-up activity to a more advanced experiential learning exercise. It works best when at least two teams of four to six players are competing.

Suggested Time   60–75 minutes (a large group will take more time due to presentations)

Materials Needed   ✓ Eggs (enough for two per team; have extras)
✓ A roll of half-inch masking tape
✓ A box of plastic drinking straws (250)
✓ A plastic garbage bag (all drops should occur on the bag)
✓ *(optional)* Flip charts for group presentations
✓ Form A (State-of-the-Art Delivery System Instructions)
✓ Form B (Materials Request Form)
✓ Form C (Team Roles)
✓ One envelope for each team

Procedure   1. The teams should be given a short explanation of what to do. The explanation should be brief and in line with the theme of the event.

"We're going to start with a little warm-up exercise to see how well you can perform as a team. The task you'll be asked to accomplish is in the envelope."

2. Put Forms A, B, and C in an envelope for each team. Place the envelopes in locations that separate the teams, if possible. (Separate rooms would be even better.) Send the teams to the locations to start the task. *Tell them that they have 45 minutes to prepare.*

3. Be available to answer questions. Teams may want to design a device that is not free falling. You should use your judgment here based on what you are trying to get from the exercise. (One group made a bungey cord from straws, which was allowed because of the "out-of-the box" thinking that the team displayed. Breakthrough thinking was a main point to the overall workshop that day.)

4. During this planning time, take notes about the team dynamics that are occuring (to be used during the debriefing).

5. During this time, teams will request materials to build their devices. Set up a "self-service materials depot." Use an honor system and let the teams track expenses on Form B.

6. Emphasize to the teams how important the presentation is to the overall project. If all the systems do not work, the presentation may be the winning vehicle.

7. Start the presentations after 45 minutes. While the presentations are going on, act as the customer awarding the contract.

8. Award points according to the following schedule:

   ✓ 50 points for any successful design

   ✓ 20 points to the team that used the least amount of materials

   ✓ 30 points for the quality of the presentation

   (*Note:* Winning the contract is important to provide motivation during the exercise, yet teams can feel they have failed if they do not win. Minimize the loss by praising the ingenuity of every team. Highlight the positive aspects of the event. The debriefing is the key to learning in the exercise.)

9. Ask the teams to return to their previous locations. Use any of the following questions to stimulate the team's reflection and learning about the experience.

   ✓ What problems did you experience as a team?

   ✓ How would you rate your teamwork on a scale of 1 to 10?

   ✓ Was there a leader who organized the team?

   ✓ Were you successful (or was your team successful)? Why or why not?

   ✓ What strengths did you bring to the team?

   ✓ What contributions did you appreciate?

✓ Did all members participate? Did any dominate?

✓ What would you change and why?

✓ Did the team members support each other?

10. Reconvene the entire group. Add your own observations of the team dynamics that you witnessed. Then conduct a closing discussion using the following questions:

✓ Can you relate this exercise to your back-on-the-job experiences as a team?

✓ What have you learned from this exercise?

✓ What can your team learn from this to carry into the next activity?

STATE-OF-THE-ART DELIVERY SYSTEM INSTRUCTIONS

You are a project team designing a state-of-the-art delivery system for dropping an egg 8 feet onto a hard surface without breaking. Other competitors are vying for the $30 million contract, to be awarded on the following criteria:

1. A fail-safe delivery system that meets the 8 foot requirement (50 points)
2. Using the least amount of materials possible (20 points)
3. A quality 5-minute presentation of your system that includes:
   - ✓ Name of your delivery system
   - ✓ Distinctive features
   - ✓ Demonstration of how your system works

   (up to 30 points)

Note:

1. Scientists have concluded that dropping eggs 8 feet eliminates cholesterol, which could revolutionize the chicken farming industry. Your company needs this contract to stay in business and many jobs depend on your efforts.
2. All drops are to be performed on a plastic bag!

MATERIALS REQUEST FORM

Team name:

Product name:

	Straws 20/pack $100	Tape (30 inches max.) $200/inch	Eggs 3 max. $5000
Original request			
Additional			
Actuals			
Cost (each)			
Total cost (actual × cost)			

Assign any these roles to members of your team:

Facilitator: _____

Project leader: _____

Design coordinator: _____

Construction coordinator: _____

Presenter: _____

Demonstrator: _____

GETTING TO KNOW YOU: A CROSS-FUNCTIONAL TEAM EXPERIENCE

Beverly Arsht and Nancy Aronson

Beverly Arsht, *Ed.D., and* **Nancy Aronson,** *Ph.D., have been consultants to educational, community, governmental, health care, business, and voluntary organizations since 1980. Their firm, Arsht/Aronson (285 Highview Drive, Wayne, PA 19087, 610-296-7354), helps to build the organization or community's internal capacity to manage and sustain the change process. Together, Nancy and Beverly plan and lead organizational interventions, coach facilitators, and offer experiences in team development. In recent years, they have facilitated numerous future search conference processes, which engage diverse, system-wide involvement in creating a shared future. Both are members of SearchNet, a nonprofit group dedicated to community service, learning, and colleagueship among future search practitioners.*

Overview   This activity gives members of various departments within an organization an initial opportunity to network and share information. It helps to create norms around tapping the resources of others and people learning from each other. *Getting to Know You* can be used when cross-functional teams are being formed or on any other occasion when representatives from different departments in an organization meet.

Suggested Time   35 minutes to 1 hour, depending on group size

Materials Needed   ✓ Form A (Getting to Know You: Instructions)
✓ Form B (Information about Me and Others)

Procedure   1. Distribute Form A to participants and use it to review the purposes and instructions for the activity.

2. If no intact crossfunctional team is present, form groups of three to six with representation across departments. (These groups can be predetermined to ensure a diverse mix of perspectives.)

3. Have participants fill out the information on Form B.

4. After 5 minutes of individual work time, have the groups begin the sharing process. Suggest that the role of timekeeper be rotated.

5. When everyone has had a turn, make sure participants take several minutes to reflect on the last question on Form B. Then invite participants to share the patterns or themes that have emerged.

Variations:

1. If participants are attending in departmental teams, form the sharing groups with representatives from across the teams. After the sharing, have departmental team members regroup to share what they have heard and identify one or two possibilities for implementation and follow-up. If time allows, ask each team to briefly summarize key points from its discussions on flip chart paper and report out to the whole group.

2. Vary the questions to make them apply directly to issues that the team or organization as a whole might be facing.

3. Use this activity across organizations.

The following activity offers you multiple opportunities to interact with those you have not worked with before. Now you have the chance to build relationships and learn from others within your organization who have information and ideas to share.

Procedure

1. Think about the first three questions found on Form B.

2. Jot down notes to yourself for questions 1 through 3.

3. Take turns sharing the information that you have written down. Each person has 10 minutes. During your 10 minutes, share your informtion, then give others the opportunity to ask you questions to clarify what you are reporting and to remark on key points that stand out for them.

4. As other people share, fill in question 4.

5. After everyone in your group has had a turn sharing, fill in question 5.

1. How would you describe your job and the role you play within your department and the organization as a whole?

2. What has been done in your department that is innovative, forward thinking, and successful (or that you feel good about)?

3. What has been done within your department to build teams and/or enhance collaboration with others?

(To be completed as you hear from the others in your group.)

4. What have you heard being done elsewhere that might be of interest to your own department?

(To be completed after everyone has taken a turn sharing information.)

5. Think about all that has been said in your group about innovation and collaboration. What patterns or themes can you identify and/or what connections can you make?

DESERT NATIONS: A CONFLICT RESOLUTION SIMULATION

Ilene Dyller

Ilene Dyller *is the president of Appleseed Consulting (6635 McCallum St., #B707, Philadelphia, PA 19119, 215-438-9218, imdyller@aol.com), an organizational consulting firm specializing in conflict resolution, team and organizational development, and health issues training. She is also a health educator dedicated to improving public health through increasing communication between health professionals and consumers. Ilene has practiced conflict mediation both in the United States and abroad.*

Overview   This activity gives team members a feeling for the complexity of conflict situations by using international conflict as an example. It exposes the long-standing distrust that often gets in the way of peace negotiations. If this simulation is used at the beginning of a team-building or organizational conflict workshop, it is very unlikely that the participants will devise workable solutions. This may set the stage for presentation and exploration of conflict resolution techniques.

Suggested Time   40 minutes

Materials Needed   ✓ Form A (Information for the Aridelphian Delegates)
    ✓ Form B (Information for the Dry Hopian Delegates)

Procedure   1. Tell the participants that this exercise will give them the opportunity to explore some of the complexities of team and organization conflict.

    2. Read the following information to the participants (give them a copy to follow):

    Aridelphia and Dry Hope are neighboring desert nations. After many years of war, the boundaries between the two are unclear. The Tiger River is the main source of water for both nations. Some people would say that the Tiger forms a natural border between the two nations. At this point, each nation claims ownership of the river, and each has armed soldiers "defending" it. As a result, thousands of people, both civilians and soldiers, have died.

Each nation needs the water from the Tiger. Aridelphia is an industrial society and needs water to keep its factories running. If Aridelphia did not have access to the water from the Tiger, factories would close and the nation's economy would break down. The nation would be unable to import food, and hundreds of thousands of people would die of hunger, thirst, and disease. On the other hand, if Aridelphia could redirect the waters of the Tiger, its economy would boom and the standard of living would go up for all.

Dry Hope is a poor agricultural nation without the necessary resources to restructure its economy. Without the water of the Tiger, crops will not grow and hundreds of thousands of people will die of hunger, thirst, and disease. Even with free access to the Tiger, the country would barely be able to feed its citizens. But, if the people of Dry Hope could redirect the river, much more of the land could be used for production. Life expectancies and health would benefit immediately, unemployment would go down, and within years Dry Hope could improve its economy tremendously and possibly even become a force in the world market.

The fighting between the two countries has intensified over the last two years and too many people have died. Both nations are under international pressure to end the war. You are here to negotiate a peace treaty.

3. Divide the team in half and assign one group to be the Aridelphian negotiators and the other to be the Dry Hopian delegation. If there are more than 10 participants, create two groups of Aridelphians and two of Dry Hopians. Give the Dry Hopians *Form A* and the Aridelphians *Form B*. Instruct them to read their forms.

4. Tell the groups that they can use whatever negotiation tactics they think will work and that they have 20 minutes.

5. After 20 minutes, interrupt the negotiations and process the exercise. Start by telling each side what the other side's instructions said. Then ask the following questions:

   ✓ Did your side want peace?

   ✓ Did you hammer out a treaty? If so, was it satisfactory to both sides?

   ✓ What tactics did you use?

   ✓ If you did not hammer out a treaty, what got in the way?

   ✓ What other tactics might you have tried?

   ✓ In what ways was this situation similar to other kinds of conflict situations that you have experienced in teams and organizations?

Variations:

1. At the end of the workshop, present a similarly difficult task as an opportunity for skill practice.

2. Before processing the exercise, reverse roles and let participants experience the concerns of the other side.

1. *You want peace.* This war is sapping your financial resources and killing your citizens. You are more than willing to be reasonable, but you *must* defend your nation's water rights at all costs.

2. *Your opponents cannot be trusted.* Twelve years ago they redirected the river onto their own land. The suffering in your country was terrible; tens of thousands died of starvation and illness, and thousands more died in the battles that followed. You won those battles and claimed the land up to the river. You would have conquered them once and for all, but you bowed to international pressure and negotiated a peace treaty. Peace was short-lived, however. As soon as you redirected the river back to its original course, the Dry Hopians attacked. They illegally annexed the land all the way up to the river. If they have their way, they will redirect the river again, and hundreds of thousands will die. *You cannot let that happen.*

3. The Dry Hopians do not care about peace. First, they are receiving weapons from a large, aggressive nation and can thus afford to keep fighting. If you did not have allies, you would have lost this war long ago. Second, they believe that they have a historical claim to the river dating back thousands of years, long before they were a country. They will not budge on this belief. What the Dry Hopians really want is to take over your nation. With your industrial strength and their agricultural strength, they would be the most powerful nation in the region.

1. *You want peace.* This war is sapping your financial resources and killing your citizens. You are more than willing to be reasonable, but you *must* defend your nation's water rights at all cost.

2. *Your opponents cannot be trusted.* The last time you negotiated peace they unilaterally redirected the river onto their own land. The suffering in your country was terrible; tens of thousands died of starvation and illness, and thousands more died in the battles that followed. You won those battles and claimed the land up to the river. Now they may want that land back, but if you give it to them, your country will no longer have access to water. *You cannot afford to let that happen.*

3. The Aridelphians do not care about peace. First, they are receiving weapons from a large, aggressive nation and can thus afford to keep fighting. If you did not have allies, you would have lost this war long ago. Second, they believe this war to be a holy cause. In their religion, it is an honor to die in a holy war, so their soldiers do not mind fighting. What they really want is to take over your nation. With your agricultural strength and their industrial strength, they would be the most powerful nation in the region.

WRAPPING IT UP: A TEAM EXERCISE

Brenda Gardner and Sharon Korth

Brenda S. Gardner, *Ph.D., is assistant professor and director of the executive Human Resource Development graduate program at Xavier University (3800 Victory Parkway, Cincinnati, OH 45207-6521, 513-745-4287, gardner@xavier.xu.edu). She is on the board of the Academy of HRD and has extensive experience in training and organization development in public and private organizations.* **Sharon J. Korth,** *Ed.D., is assistant professor of HRD at Xavier University (513-745-4276, korth@xavier.xu.edu). She has chapters in* **In Action: Conducting Needs Assessment,** *edited by Jack Phillips and Elwood Holton (Alexandria, VA: ASTD, 1995) and* **ASTD Toolkit: More Needs Assessment Instruments,** *edited by John Wilcox (Alexandria, VA: American Society for Training and Development, 1994).*

Overview   This exercise will provide participants with a light experience to learn about organizational communication patterns and team problem solving. The processing of this exercise can be adapted in many ways to introduce or reinforce the main learning points of a longer training module. (The exercise can be particularly fun if used in a training session near a holiday season.)

Suggested Time   40–50 minutes

Material Needed   ✓ *For each small group:* A roll of wrapping paper, roll of cellophane tape, pair of right-handed scissors, roll of ribbon, empty box (all hidden from view of participants until needed)

✓ *For each observer:* Form A

✓ *For each coach:* Form B

✓ *For each wrapper:* Cloth blindfold and Form C

Procedure

1. Break the large group of participants into small groups of at least six to eight. If the objective of the exercise is team building, the small groups should be composed of intact work groups.

2. Each group should remain standing around a table large enough to hold all materials. Designate three wrappers, two to three coaches, and one to two observers in each group, using a random selection

process such as "The three persons whose birthdays fall latest in the year are wrappers," then "of those persons remaining, the two who traveled the farthest to get to the training session are coaches," and "the remaining participants are observers."

3. With the group members standing around their table, give the wrappers cloth blindfolds with instructions to put them on. Then place the set of wrapping materials in the middle of each table.

4. Read the following instructions to participants.

   The goal of this exercise is for each group to wrap and put a ribbon on a gift box, in a quality and timely fashion.

   Observers, please read this form I'm handing out to you (hand out Form A) and observe the exercise without interacting with either the wrappers or coaches.

   Coaches, you are allowed to provide verbal instructions and feedback to the wrappers, but cannot touch the wrappers or the materials on the table.

   *Wrappers, all the materials that you need to wrap and tie your gift are on the table. You are allowed to communicate verbally with your group's coaches. Each group of wrappers can communicate with each other and use any means to accomplish the task, but you must keep your blindfolds on and **only use your nonpreferred hands to wrap and tie your gift**.*

   So, wrappers, place your preferred hand behind your back, and ready, set, go!

5. Depending on your objective, stop the exercise when one group has finished wrapping and tying the gift and judge the wrapping as being of sufficient quality. Or the exercise can be continued until all groups finish their tasks, and a judging contest can be held to designate which team of wrappers did the best job.

6. Hand out Form B's to coaches and Form C's to wrappers. Have all coaches, wrappers and observers individually complete their respective forms (5 to 7 minutes).

7. Have each small group share among themselves their responses to the questions on their forms (15 minutes).

8. In a large group, ask each small group to briefly report the results of their discussion. Record key points on flip charts.

9. Ask the participants to identify how their learning could be transferred to on-the-job situations. Summarize the participants' comments in relationship to your original objectives, that is, organizational communication, team problem solving, and the like.

Variations:

1. Additional rules can be given to emphasize various learning points:

   One-way communication issues: Change the rules so that the wrappers cannot ask questions of the coaches.

Leadership and communication issues: Change the rules so that the wrappers choose a leader, the coaches choose a leader, and only the leaders can communicate with each across groups.

2. This exercise can be conducted with the objective to increase awareness of the issues involved in supervising and training physically challenged or older employees. For example, you could add physical constraints to the wrappers, such as gloved hands, vaseline-smeared glasses, or wheelchairs.

While you are observing the group's task, use this form to jot down notes about their process:

1. Did the group of coaches make a plan to communicate with the wrappers? If so, how did they decide? Did the strategy work? Did the strategy change? If they didn't decide on a particular strategy, why not?

2. Did the group of wrappers decide on a particular strategy to communicate with the coaches? If so, how did they decide? Did the strategy work? Did the strategy change? If they didn't decide on a particular strategy, why not?

3. Were there particular behaviors in the group of coaches that helped the wrappers accomplish their task? Describe them.

4. Were there particular behaviors in the group of coaches that hindered the wrappers in accomplishing their task? Describe them.

5. Were there particular behaviors in the group of wrappers that helped them accomplish their task? Describe them.

6. Were there particular behaviors in the group of wrappers that hindered their accomplishing their task? Describe them.

1. How did it feel to be able to give verbal instructions but not have eye contact or be able to help the wrappers to physically manipulate their task?

2. Did your group of coaches decide on a particular strategy to communicate with the wrappers? If so, how did you decide? Did the strategy work? Did the strategy change? If you didn't decide on a particular strategy, why not?

3. Were there particular behaviors in your group of coaches or within the group of wrappers that helped the wrappers accomplish their task? Describe them.

4. Were there particular behaviors that hindered your group of coaches in their task? Describe them.

5. Looking back, are there changes you would make in your process? What might they be?

QUESTIONS FOR WRAPPERS

1. How did it feel to be able to receive verbal instructions but not have eye or physical contact with your coaches?

2. Did your group of wrappers decide on a particular strategy to communicate with the coaches? If so, how did you decide? Did the strategy work? Did the strategy change? If you didn't decide on a particular strategy, why not?

3. Were there particular behaviors in the group of coaches or within your group of wrappers that helped you to accomplish your task? Describe them.

4. Were there particular behaviors that hindered accomplishing your task? Describe them.

5. Looking back, are there changes you would make in your process? What might they be?

"I'M ALL FOR IT!"
AN ORGANIZATIONAL
COMMITMENT EXERCISE

Cathleen Hutchison

Cathleen Smith Hutchison *is managing partner of Conifer Consulting Group (PO Box 1147, Cedar Crest, NH 87008, 505-281-4496), a full-service human resource consulting firm specializing in managing corporate change including change components such as culture change and re-engineering. She is a past officer of the National Society for Performance and Instruction at national and chapter levels and of the International Board of Standards for Training, Performance and Instruction.*

Overview
In today's fast changing business environment, many initiatives within an organization require demonstrated commitment from managers throughout the organization. However, there is often a lack of clarity about what demonstrates commitment. This is especially perplexing because commitment is an internal state of mind. What does a manager need to do or say to demonstrate commitment? This exercise addresses these issues.

The goals of this exercise are to clarify and identify the observable behaviors that demonstrate the internal state of commitment. A second portion of the exercise may be used to identify specific behaviors that each manager will take to demonstrate his or her commitment to a specific initiative within the organization. The activity can often be used to advantage at the end of a program introducing a new corporate initiative. It also makes an effective transition from discussion of an initiative to taking action to support it.

Suggested Time
30–45 minutes (a very large group could run somewhat longer)

Materials Needed
✓ Flip chart pad and easel
✓ Markers
✓ Post-it™ pads (large size)
✓ Pens for participants
✓ Form A (Key Actions and Characteristics of Commitment)

✓ Form B (Key Concept Reading: Commitment)

✓ Form C (Individual Exercise: Personal Commitments)

Procedure *This training activity is in two parts. Although each can be conducted independently, there is greater impact when they are conducted together.*

Part I

1. Distribute Form A to participants.

2. Ask participants to read the directions and complete the worksheet. Give them 5 minutes to do so. Distribute pens as needed.

3. Ask several participants to share their examples.

4. As they do so, write words that summarize their descriptive actions and characteristics on the flip chart. Prompt the group by asking questions such as "What did you see them do that showed you that they were committed?"

5. Chart several actions and/or characteristics that can be categorized into each of the four areas of "frequency," "energy level," "level of risk or personal sacrifice," and "level of accountability and personal responsibility," as decribed in Form B.

6. Lead a discussion on the similarities between what is observed in the variety of examples that have been shared (5 minutes). Help the group to reach categorizations of similarities that approximate the four areas listed in step 5.

7. Next, list the four areas on a flip chart. Distribute Form B and ask participants to read it. Seek group consensus that these areas represent what they have described in their examples.

8. Ask if there are any other areas that should be listed and chart any additions.

9. Lead a group discussion on commitment and the implications for the participants in demonstrating their commitment to the specific corporate initiative. Ensure that all key points made in the concept reading (Form B) are made about the meaning of each of the four areas.

10. Ask the group for sample actions that might represent the individual's commitment to this specific corporate initiative.

Part II

11. Distribute Form C to participants.

12. Distribute Post-it™ pads and pens as needed.

13. Give participants 5 minutes to read the directions and write out their commitments. Remind participants to sign them legibly.

14. Ask participants to come forward, read their commitments aloud to the group, and post them on the wall or a blank flip chart page. Continue until all participants have been heard from.

15. Charge all participants to hold themselves and their fellow participants accountable for the commitments that they have made to support this specific corporate initiative.

16. Collect all commitments and have them typed up with the names of the participants next to what they have committed to. Share the list of all commitments with all participants. (This can be during a program or as a follow-up reminder a week or so after the program.)

Variation:

A large group may be divided into small groups to conduct steps 3 through 6. Then the large group reconvenes and the small groups debrief their discussions. The discussion in smaller teams tends to become more poignant and meaningful, particularly if they are conducted in small breakout rooms. Be aware, however, that the examples given may also become more emotional and personal in a small group.

KEY ACTIONS AND CHARACTERISTICS
OF COMMITMENT

Purpose

In this exercise, you will be discussing how to make the internal state of commitment an observable set of behaviors.

Step 1: Think of a time when someone you know was highly committed to accomplishing something. Examples can come from your friends and family and personal life or from your work experience. What did you see them do?

a. Describe the situation.

b. List the key actions and characteristics that you observed.

Step 2: Discuss with your group the actions and characteristics you wrote down in step 1.

✓ Are there consistent elements from all, or many of, the stories that the group tells?

✓ Are there other things that you can do to make your internal commitment observable to others?

List the key actions and characteristics that you observed.

Commitment is an enigmatic concept. It is a state of being that exists inside the individual being observed. Many things can contribute to whether it is perceived by others, but it cannot be directly observed. It depends solely on the observance of secondary actions and characteristics.

An individual can, conceivably, be highly committed to making something happen, but feel very negative about the likelihood that it will happen. In some individuals, this negativism and cynicism may overshadow their commitment in the perceptions of others.

The key ways that people judge another individual's level of commitment to something are the following:

✓ *Frequency* of discussions and/or actions around the issue

✓ *Energy level* displayed when involved in discussion and/or actions around the issue

✓ *Level of risk and/or personal sacrifice* that the individual is willing to make because of the issue

✓ *Level of accountability and personal responsibility* that the individual takes for seeing that contributing steps are accomplished

Frequency

People are generally drawn to those things to which they give high value. If they are committed to accomplishing something, it is usually something that they value for one reason or another. Therefore, they want to and/or do spend time involved with that issue or activity. A would-be athlete who is committed to making the team spends many hours practicing. Think of the movie *Rocky* and the amount of time spent in practice and preparation for the big fight. He made training for the fight his life's work.

Energy Level

There is frequently a level of passion around a cause or issue to which an individual is committed. Individuals frequently display animated expressions and/or more energetic gestures when they are describing something to which they are passionately committed. Rightly or wrongly, we tend to expect to see a heightened level of energy as a signal of commitment.

Some individuals are very low key. They may never display much animation or energy. The risk for our expectation of a high energy level as a signal of commitment is that it does not show up in every individual.

Level of Risk and/or Personal Sacrifice

We also associate an individual's willingness to take risks or make some level of personal sacrifice with his or her level of commitment. The most common examples that we encounter involve dieting and quitting smoking. You can hear someone say that they have to lose weight or they need to quit smoking almost every day. We recognize that those who are truly committed to accomplishing these goals must forego that piece of pie or must endure that craving for a cigarette. Without making such "small sacrifices," the weight will never be lost or the cigarettes given up.

The same is frequently true of accomplishing a business mission or vision. There may be late nights or weekends at work when you would rather be spending time with family or friends. There may be a trip out of town at an inopportune time. There may be a decision that must be made with incomplete information or an action that must be taken that could backfire or blow up if mishandled. Perhaps other priorities must be allowed to slip in order to achieve this one.

We expect that individuals who are committed will make these sacrifices and take these risks. We unconsciously tie personal sacrifice so closely to commitment that if sacrifice is not necessary we may not recognize that commitment exists.

Accountability has two components. One is the level of personal responsibility and accountability that the individual takes on for himself or herself. The other is the level of accountability that the individual expects from others. The two go hand in hand.

Being accountable and taking responsibility require believing that you are in charge of your own behavior. When you make decisions and take action, you must be willing to be accountable for what you have undertaken. This does not mean that you do not sometimes err or fail, for if you never fail you are not setting your targets very high. You are being accountable for your own actions when you are willing to take constructive risks and accept the consequences.

At the same time, someone who is committed to accomplishing something will not easily accept excuses from others for not completing their portions of the project. They hold others as accountable as they hold themselves. Committed individuals are willing to help others work through barriers to achieve their outcomes, but they are not willing to accept others' unwillingness to try and to make personal sacrifices also.

When someone is committed to a group goal, she or he expects all members of the group to be equally committed. This translates to an expectation that all members will be accountable for and take personal responsibility for their own actions.

Personal responsibility and commitment by all employees are critical to an organization's ability to be competitive. Individuals in a position to be aware of an opportunity or need for improvement either take action and improve the organization's competitive position or they do not take action and they decrease the organization's competitive position. It is that simple and that complex.

If everyone in the organization steps up to the challenges, the organization's position improves. If just one individual ignores an identified opportunity or need, then the organization is not as competitive as it could be.

INDIVIDUAL EXERCISE: PERSONAL COMMITMENTS

Purpose

In this exercise you will be making a personal commitment to action.

List 1 or 2 things that you personally can do and will commit to doing within the next 30 to 90 days to support [a specific corporate initiative].

Write them each on an individual Post-it™ note and sign your name legibly. Be prepared to read your commitment aloud to the large group.

Notes

_____

_____

_____

_____

_____

_____

_____

_____

_____

_____

A TEAM-BUILDING OLYMPICS: LET THE GAMES BEGIN

Jeanne Baer

Jeanne Baer *is president of Creative Training Solutions (1649 South 21st Street, Lincoln, NE 68502, 800-410-3178, jbaer@grex.cyberspace.org). The company provides training, facilitation, and program design services to clients as diverse as Chrysler, Burlington Northern, IDS, the International Festivals Association, and the Travel Industry Association of America. She teaches at Southeast Community College, writes for* **Training Media Review,** *and is a past president of the Lincoln, Nebraska, chapter of the American Society for Training and Development.*

Overview

Often, one of the most important goals for a team-building retreat is to provide a way for participants to get to know each other better or to *bond*. An Olympic-style competition is an excellent way to achieve this goal. Like the true Olympics, your event can offer pageantry, color, excitement, and teamwork. However, yours departs from that world-renowned event in several ways: one need not be athletic to win, some of the events are silly, no injuries are anticipated, and cooperation replaces competition in your Olympics' final event.

Effective for groups of 15 to 300, your Olympics features fun events for people of all sizes, ages, and abilities. The events give people a chance to get to know each other in a nonwork setting and requires true team-work to win.

Suggested Time

Open to several choices

Materials Needed

See details later

Procedure

Overall Design

1. The first thing to do is plan the individual events that will constitute your Olympics. Consider the following sample events:

   ✓ *Overachiever's First Aid:* This safety lesson will give four team members plenty of practice bandaging. The assumption is that one team member has three paper cuts—one on each hand and one on his or her forehead. Three teammates must wrap the cut fingers and head with about 20 feet of bandages, tucking the ends of the bandages in neatly. When a team finishes and its bandages are okayed by judges, the three bandagers remove the bandages, and a second team member is bandaged by the other three. Again the bandaging is okayed, after which the third and finally the fourth member are wrapped up. The first team to bandage all its members wins.

✓ *Collator's Nightmare:* The starter tosses a huge pile of various-colored, numbered sheets of paper into the air (40 for each team). The task facing each team of six athletes is to pick up the sheets in their assigned color and collate them in numerical order! The first team to finish wins.

✓ *Linking Up:* Athletes have 3 minutes to take large, colorful paper clips from a pile and link them into a chain. Since the three-member teams can only use one hand, teamwork is important! The longest chain wins.

✓ *Forms Management 101 (Wastebasket Basketball):* Working together in teams of five, the first player crumples a "form" into a ball, and it is thrown to the next player, and to the third, fourth, and finally to the fifth, who shoots it into a wastebasket. The team that scores the most baskets within 5 minutes wins.

✓ *Doughnut and Java Juggle:* Athletes must run with a cup of "coffee" (water) in both hands and a doughnut on a drinking straw, relay style. When they reach a teammate, they transfer the doughnut to the teammates' awaiting straw and transfer the coffee. The process is repeated to a third and a fourth teammate. First team to return (with doughnut intact) is the winner.

2. The last event of the Olympics should give participants a chance to work with each other instead of competing against each other and should involve all participants. Here's one possibility called *The Big Picture:*

✓ For this closing event, each athlete gets one or more giant jigsaw puzzle pieces, and must work with everyone to assemble the puzzle. The goal? To see the "big picture" as soon as possible!

✓ To produce The Big Picture, construct a giant jigsaw puzzle with an inspiring message on it. It might be the organization's mission or vision statement or a slogan such as, "We can't spell s ccess without U!" (*Note:* "Giant" really does mean very large. Four feet by eight feet is not too large to be considered a workable minimum.)

✓ Decide on the message and accompanying artwork. Transfer it to the material you have chosen for the puzzle. If you intend to use the puzzle repeatedly, consider constructing it out of ⅛-inch plywood. If not, corrugated cardboard is a good choice.

✓ Next, cut into interlocking pieces. You may cut it into the number of participants you are expecting, or you can cut it into many pieces and invite everyone to fit as many pieces as possible.

✓ If you want the event to go more quickly, you can number pieces sequentially and tell participants to find people with numbers close to theirs. Or you can label some pieces "top row," "bottom row," and so on.

✓ One option is to instruct participants that they must put the puzzle together without talking to each other. That way, you can later do a process observation about what behaviors did and did not work well, leading to some insights about teamwork and communication.

✓ Another option is to run the event twice; first without talking and then with talking. Time both tries so that participants can see how much faster they accomplish the goal when they are able to fully communicate.

✓ Regardless of how you conduct the event, be sure that everyone receives a prize for participating.

Planning Considerations

3. When you are brainstorming event possibilities, consider whether your Olympics will be indoors, outdoors with a hard surface, or outdoors on a grassy surface; some events may require a particular surface or setting. You will want to have diverse events calling on a variety of abilities and knowledge; while some events may call for speed or agility, not all should. Where possible, make success contingent on members working together as a team. Your final event should be one that brings the entire group together, competing not against each other, but against the clock.

4. The number of events that you organize depends on the total amount of time that you have available. Estimate the amount of time it will take to run any given event and then to award prizes for it. If you cannot set up for one event until you complete the previous one, you will also have to build in setup time.

5. You will also need to think about the number of athletes from each team that you want to participate in each event. This will depend on the amount of space you have, the amount of supplies and prizes that you want to provide, and the amount of time that you want to take for the event.

6. Be sure to have enough athletes competing in each event, and/or organize enough different events so that everyone can participate as much as possible. (While athletes are involved in an event, their remaining teammates should be nearby, cheering them on.)

7. Another factor in your selection or invention of games is the supplies required to run them. To keep the cost reasonable, use supplies you can borrow and return versus those you must buy and use up or have

to store. Thrift stores can be an excellent source of some supplies. Create events that are especially appropriate to your industry. Often slight modifications of games you already know, accompanied by some creative descriptions, will customize them cleverly. You can also create a quiz bowl-style event, with silly and serious questions about the organization or any body of knowledge that you want to spotlight.

8. Decide whether you wish to do process observations on some, all, or none of the events. My personal preference is to debrief only the last event in this way. If too much process observing takes place, it slows the pace of the Olympics and can sap the energy of participants.

9. Some planning in each of the following areas is required. Just how much detail is needed will be determined by your own Olympics.

Creating Teams

10. The more teams you have, the more unwieldy the games become in terms of setup, supplies, and prizes. Three to six teams are easy, eight teams become a challenge, and any more than ten, a real headache. Each team should be made up of 5 to 20 members. In advance, decide who will be on what teams, making up teams of equal or nearly equal size. Assign each team a color, and instruct members to decide on a name to accompany their color (for example, the Green Giants, the Red Raiders, the Turquoise Tornadoes). This can be done before the Olympics in a promotional mailing or once the participants arrive for the retreat. At the site of the competition, create "camps" for each team by gathering chairs around team tables. If your budget permits, provide bandannas or T-shirts in team colors so that it will be easy to identify the members of each team.

Advance Promotion

11. Promote the games in advance to build anticipation and interest. If the purpose of the games is to organize a friendly competition among already existing divisions, regions, or other groups, promotion is especially important. Also, if you make your Olympics sound too frivolous, some people will resist participating. Therefore, make your promotional mailing(s) fun, energetic, and creative, but also purposeful, promising a useful perspective on the skills that ensure successful teamwork.

Before the Games Begin

12. Before the Olympics officially starts, you will want to allow some time for team bonding. Coming up with their own team name, a team chant or song, and even a team flag are some possibilities.

13. The Olympics often take place after a meal. That way, athletes can begin to build esprit de corps while or right after they eat. Give each team a balloon bouquet in its team color and have participants decide on a team name. You may wish to supply felt-tip pens so that they can write the name on the balloons.

14. You may also invite them to come up with a slogan, chant, or very short song. That way, when their team wins an event, they can shout or sing it in unison, roughly equivalent to the playing of an Olympic winner's national anthem. To simplify song writing, assign each team a different, well-known tune, such as "Old McDonald." They only need to come up with a few lyrics to fit it.

15. Another option is to have each team make and fly its own flag. Provide each team with felt-tip pens in many colors, along with a large piece of white fabric or poster board. Also provide a stick that they can attach it to and a way to display the flags once the teams get them to the competition site.

Prizes

16. Award prizes to first-place teams. If you have many teams, sufficient funding, and the time to gather lots of prizes, award second and third prizes also. Silly prizes are often appreciated more than a serious prize would be. Specialty advertising companies can help you with imaginative prizes, and a company like Oriental Trading (800-228-2269) has thousands of inexpensive items. If your budget is more limited than your time, lead a shopping expedition to nearby thrift stores.

17. Try to select prizes that tie into each event. For instance, for "Overachiever's First Aid" you might award boxes of neon-colored "Band-aids," and for the "Big Picture" you might award magnifying glasses. Another option is to award Olympic-style medals for each event. You can find gold, silver, and bronze medals hung on red, white, and blue ribbons at trophy shops.

Ambience

18. You can set an Olympics mood with some imaginative music and decor.

19. Erect large posters declaring, "Welcome World-Class Athletes!" or "Welcome to the _____-Lympics!" (combining the name of your organization with the word Olympics).

20. To further carry out the theme, spray-paint five hula hoops in the Olympics colors, wire them together in the Olympic rings configuration, and hang them prominently. Decorate with many brightly colored helium-filled balloons, preferably in colors not already assigned to teams.

21. Heroic-sounding, "epic"-style music should be played at the beginning and the end of the Olympics and may be played throughout.

Olympic Pageantry

22. You may wish to begin your Olympics with a parade of the athletes. They can march in with their flags and/or balloons, accompanied by Olympic-style music provided by a hired marching band or by tape.

Music might include John Williams' "Olympic Fanfare" (recorded by the Cincinnati Pops on the Telark label) or Leo Armaud's "Olympic Fanfare" (part of "Bugler's Dream," recorded by The Concert Arts Symphonic Band, conducted by Felix Slatkin on the Angel LP "USA" label). Music from the film *Chariots of Fire* would be another good choice. For liability's sake, check with ASCAP or other licensing bodies and pay the required fees for using these pieces.

23. If teams have written a chant, slogan, or song, they can now perform them for the other teams. You or an Olympics "official" then welcomes the athletes, and then, "Let the games begin!"

24. If teams have created their own team chant, slogan, or song, you might invite the winning team to perform it when the prizes are given for each event. The entire team should be encouraged to perform, not just the athletes who competed in this event.

Logistics

25. To help your Olympics run smoothly, you will need to pay attention to various details. As you can imagine, the number of details grows as the number of people grows. The following issues and questions are ones to consider:

Logo: Will you want a special logo designed to print on promotional materials, prizes, and uniforms? If so, start developing it *early*; allow adequate time for the approval process and for printing it on items.

Team uniforms: Will you identify team athletes with color-coded T-shirts or bandannas? Can you get them in the correct colors and sizes? Will they be printed?

Balloon bouquets: Can they be delivered by a balloon company, or must you rent a tank of helium and fill them at the site? After the Olympics are over, will the balloons be donated or will they be kept by participants?

Insurance: Are you covered for possible injuries?

Security: Is someone available to keep passers-by from joining in? While this is rarely a problem indoors, it can be if your Olympics are held in a public park.

Refreshments: Will you be providing light snacks and beverages? Will someone be needed to serve them or to be sure that the supply is continuous? If you don't provide them, are vending machines nearby?

Getting participants' attention: Do you have a public address system or bull horns with plenty of batteries available? Athletic-style whistles?

Restrooms: Are they nearby? If you are outdoors, consider renting portable toilets to be placed near your Olympics area.

Souvenir photos: Can you afford a videographer to tape the event? If not, can you arrange for people to take still photos? Will you copy tapes or photos for participants later? What will the cost be, if any?

Helpers: Do you have two or more helpers for setup, awarding prizes, and other tasks? If you have over 100 participants, consider having a special coach (facilitator) assigned to each team. These people will keep the teams organized, enthusiastic, and where they are supposed to be when they are supposed to be there.

Inclement weather: If you plan to hold your Olympics outdoors, do you have a contingency plan for bad weather? Do you have a back-up, indoor site reserved? Do you have transportation waiting to move the whole group quickly? If you don't want to move the games inside, what will participants do if the games are canceled?

Cost

26. A team-building Olympics can be effective on almost any scale and budget. A small-scale example: an hour-long indoor Olympics for 50 participants on five teams, with supplies and prizes costing $85. A large-scale example: a 5-hour long corporate Olympics with 200 participants on 10 teams, requiring 6 months of preparation for and six additional hired facilitators, with supplies and prizes alone costing about $8000.

BRIDGE ACROSS THE AMAZON: AN EXERCISE IN TEAM PROBLEM SOLVING

Bert Nemcik

Bert Nemcik, *Ph.D., is the training director for the Abraxas Foundation (Abraxas @vaxa.clarion.edu), an adolescent alcohol or drug rehabilitation program with 17 sites in Pennsylvania, West Virginia, and Ohio. He is the founder of the Lifelong Learning Network (RD 2, Marienville, PA 16239, 814-927-5640), a private consulting firm dedicated to advancing adult learning practices. He has published 15 electronic texts covering topics such as human motivation, supervision, and adult learning. He writes a weekly newspaper column entitled* **"Life, Liberty, and Library."**

Overview   In this activity, participants will need to communicate nonverbally with one another in order to complete the task. The activity is particularly effective as a prelude to training in team problem solving. It will work with up to 10 participants. If there are more than 10, break the team into two smaller groups.

Suggested Time   40 minutes

Materials Needed   ✓ Large floor space at least 20 feet long and 10 feet wide

✓ One 4-inch by 4-inch by 16-foot beam with cross braces on the ends and center so that it will not shift when participants are on it.

Procedure   1. Before the instructions are given, the beam must be set up. If it is to be used more than once for later activities, it can be covered with outdoor carpet to make it safer.

2. Tell the participants this is an activity that will provide them the opportunity to develop their problem-solving skills.

3. If the group is larger than 10, then divide it in half by counting off 1, 2, 1, 2, ... This breaks up pairs of people who may have been sitting together and evenly divides the participants.

4. Ask the first group (if there are more than one) to get on the beam.

5. Now explain to them what they are to do with the following words:

This is a bridge stretched high across the Amazon River. The river is full of piranhas. If you fall of, you will be eaten alive. Your task is, once I give you the direction to proceed, to arrange yourselves on the bridge, from oldest to youngest by chronological age, with the oldest here on the right and the youngest on the left. (See variations for alternative instructions.) **You cannot talk with one another.** *You must communicate nonverbally. You must move around on the bridge by working with one another. If you fall off, you must begin all over again where you started. Are there any questions? If not, then begin.*

6. Stand back and permit the team to begin. Ensure that the ground rules are followed and that the activity proceeds safely. If the team is doing anything that might be considered unsafe, intervene immediately.

7. After the team successfully completes the task, ask the following questions:

   a. What strategies were used by the group to complete the task?

   b. In hindsight, can you think of other strategies that might have been more efficient?

   c. If you had time to plan how to do the task before getting on the bridge, what team problem-solving tools do you know about that could have been used?

   d. As you worked on this task, certain people assumed leadership and other roles. What happened?

   e. If you were going to undertake this activity all over again, what kinds of things would you do differently the second time?

   f. What could any team learn from this activity about team problem solving? Does this apply to your team?

Variations:

1. As the participants are struggling to arrange themselves on the beam, photograph them working with one another. Photographs can be shared with the team later as a graphic portrayal of their having worked hard to develop a strong, trusting team.

2. If the group is comprised of many physically unfit people or very large individuals, the facilitator needs to overlook their violation of the rule regarding falling off the bridge. The goal is that they complete the activity with minimal amount of rules violations.

3. If the group is comprised of many younger participants who are physically fit, then more of them can be placed on the beam at one time. This makes them work harder.

4. Instead of arranging themselves by chronological age, the following variations can be used:

a. "Arrange yourselves based upon years of service with the company, from longest to shortest, left to right on the beam."

b. "Arrange yourselves from the tallest to the shortest, right to left on the beam."

c. "Arrange yourselves by gender with women to the left and men to the right on the beam."

d. "Arrange yourselves with the person with the longest hair to the left and the shortest to the right on the beam."

e. Let the participants be creative. There are many more alternatives that they might suggest.

THE CASE OF THE MISSING INFORMATION: A NEGOTIATION ROLE PLAY

Catherine Penna

Catherine J. Penna *is a fellowship recipient at Colorado State University (cpenna@lamar.colostate.edu), currently pursuing a Ph.D. in human resource development. Catherine is an independent human resource development consultant (2516 22nd Drive, Longmont, CO, 303-772-5185) and has been a corporate trainer specializing in needs analysis and course design. She has a published paper on training transfer from the Academy of Human Resource Development and is preparing her doctoral dissertation on industry's return of investment from skills development.*

Overview This role play gives participants an opportunity to act out a situation that occurs in everyday life at work or other organizations. The activity puts people in a conflict state, one in which they were not provided all the information and invites the participants to jump to conclusions. It promotes effective communication and negotiation skills. It also gives the participants an opportunity to do a needs analysis to determine the opposing group's needs.

Suggested Time 40–60 minutes

Materials Needed ✓ Form A (Employee Role Play Information Sheet)
✓ Form B (Management Role Play Information Sheet)

Procedure 1. Introduce this role play as a needs analysis and negotiations exercise. Tell the participants that there will be two groups, one a management team and the other an employee team.

2. Divide the group in half. Give the employee team copies of Form A and the management team copies of Form B. Tell them that they have 20 minutes to prepare for their role play. Have each team prepare for this role play in separate rooms (if possible).

3. After the teams have separated, inform the employee team that they are to call a meeting with management to discuss this situation. They can do it as a group or as an individual and can call on the whole management team or just a specific member. Allow the team to decide how to do this and leave it very unstructured. Some teams may feel a level of discomfort with this, but this feeling will only enhance their ability to work out a problem in a situation where all the information regarding decisions made is not disclosed. As the facilitator, you will benefit from listening in on how this team works together and can use that information in the discussion following the role play.

4. Inform the management team that they will be approached by the employee team in some fashion. Let this group know that they may not have all the information on the day-to-day operations of the employee team. This may cause discomfort to this team because they will not know what they are dealing with, but this can occur with many activities in the organization.

5. After 20 minutes, call the teams together. Turn the attention to the employee group and let them take over the role play. Stay as uninvolved as possible, allowing the teams to work out this situation. If the teams meet an impasse, suggest items in their role play that they may have overlooked or provide alternative suggestions that they might try. Allow the teams to negotiate and perform needs analysis activities for 20 to 40 minutes, time allowing.

6. Ask the total group for feedback. How did they feel about this situation? What were their thoughts before entering into the meeting? What was their comfort level with the other group? What other tools or resources could have been used in resolving this conflict?

7. Summarize this experience. Note examples of comments that you heard while the teams were planning this encounter. Generalize this information to what happens in organizations today. Ask for examples from participants of similar situations that they have encountered.
    Mention the following steps to successful negotiation:

✓ Describe the conflict as a mutual problem.

✓ Offer to negotiate differences.

✓ Brainstorm together alternative solutions.

✓ Evaluate brainstormed solutions.

✓ Decide on the best solution.

✓ Plan how the solutions will be implemented.

Your group is employed by Ace Company and you are working in a manufacturing environment. You manufacture widgets. Your group is a very cohesive group and works extremely well together. In fact, your group has been held up as the model in teamwork for the entire company.

Lately there has been a cutback in the education and training supplied to your group. The technical skills required for the job are now acquired by on-the-job training, and any soft skills (communications, negotiations, leadership) training has been accomplished by in-house seminars, time permitting. Due to growth in the demand for widgets, there has been no informal training for 8 months.

This cutback in training has caused great concern in your group, because some of the members have been attending the graduate program at CSU and have brought back ideas on how progressive companies have a continuous-learning philosophy while maintaining profits. Your group sees this as a goal for the company and is committed to working toward that end, both for professional and personal objectives.

You have asked the management team for funding for education but have received no positive response. The reasons for the denial are unclear, which is confusing because your management has always been open and receptive to your requests.

Your job: Do a minineeds analysis to determine why the management team will not endorse the requested education. The other team is the management team.

Your group is the management team for Ace Company. You manufacture widgets. Recently you have heard from the president that the budget needs to be cut due to the growing number of competitors, all manufacturing widgets. While the need for widgets is growing, you need to cut overhead because competitors are pricing their widgets below the price that you charge.

You have analyzed your organization and have made cutbacks in several departments already. Further analysis has indicated that the training budget is rather large. Through initial inquiries, you have found that on-the-job training appears to be an effective alternative to the high cost of formal training. At some time in the past, the manufacturing group handled the need for professional training with informal seminars, but these have diminished due to productivity requirements. Recently, this group has been pressing you for time off from production so that they can resume these classes, which you feel are of little value in widget making. You are concerned that their team goals do not match those of the company.

Just yesterday, you found that the productivity requirement has been increased by 10% and a downsizing effort is underway. The manufacturing team is not aware of this.

Your job: Determine how you are going to meet the needs of your employees while meeting company objectives, keeping in mind that this team is used as a model for the company to demonstrate effective teamwork and cohesiveness.

SHARING PERSONAL VISIONS: A TEAM BUILDER

Beth Banks

Beth J. Banks *is lead trainer at Ethicon, Inc. (a Johnson & Johnson company), Box 151, Route 22 West, Somerville, NJ 08876, 908-218-2240, bjbanks829@aol.com. She specializes in computer systems implementation, team building, and change management and is the author of "Teaching from the Heart: Being a Trainer in the Age of Change" in* **End User Computer Management,** *December, 1994. She is currently a Ph.D. (human and organizational systems) student with The Fielding Institute.*

Overview   Organizations are changing: centralizing, decentralizing, flattening, matrixing. These phenomena put people together in new, challenging, and sometimes frightening relationships. Sharing a personal vision helps new groups of people who will work together to introduce their values and goals in a genuine and meaningful way. This activity could be part of a team-building session or meeting for a new team, a group crossing several departments, divisions, or companies that have merged, or a new matrix organization.

Suggested Time   60–90 minutes

Materials Needed   ✓ Form A (Vision Definitions)
✓ Form B (A Journey in Time)
✓ Paper for drawing pictures (white, heavy bond)
✓ Crayons, markers, colored pencils

Procedure   1. Introduce the concept of creating a personal vision and explain it in the context in which it will be used. You might indicate some of the following:
    ✓ A personal vision plays an important role in the vision of a team or organization. Without its members, there would be no shared visions.

69

✓ Most people already have a personal vision that includes their personal life. Most people have not taken the time to think about a personal vision for their work life, even though we spend a significant amount of time there.

✓ Reflecting on and sharing a personal vision are genuine and meaningful ways to introduce ourselves, our values, and our goals to new work colleagues.

2. Define a vision and a personal vision. Emphasize that the personal vision that each person will create during this exercise will be specific to his or her life at work. Use Peter Block's *The Empowered Manager* and Peter Senge's *The Fifth Discipline* for these definitions. See Form A for an example.

3. Acknowledge some fears that may exist for people around creating and talking about their personal vision with others, such as the following: *What if my vision is not viewed as valid? What if my vision is in conflict with others? If I say my vision out loud, I may have to accomplish it!*

4. Introduce the concept of visualization and its use in creating a personal vision. Indicate that visualization is used by many successful athletes who create "personal success visions" before an event. Explain that in order to create a vision in their minds of their ideal future, they will need to make a journey there.

Ask participants to close their eyes, relax, and listen to your voice. Explain that you will be telling them a story to help them to formulate pictures in their minds of their preferred work future. Use Form B as a basis for this visualization. Use background music if appropriate.

5. Ask participants to open their eyes. Introduce the next step, which is drawing a representation of their visions on paper. Participants will need 20 to 25 minutes to work on this. Here are ways to approach the drawing:

a. Drawing may be a huge departure from what people are used to in a work seminar. Acknowledge that this approach is different. Say something like this: *At work we spend a lot of time using the logical part of our brain. By drawing, we are trying to use the creative part. I know it is different, but let's give it a try.* Remind participants that visions are not meant to be practical, but rather a reflection of our imagination and spirit, so a picture is an appropriate way to represent it.

b. Acknowledge that most people feel that they cannot draw. Remind them that this is not a drawing contest. No one will laugh at their efforts or make fun of their picture. All efforts should be recognized as valuable reflections of themselves.

c. Emphasize that the drawing does not have to be elaborate. Participants can and should use stick figures and simple ways of representing what they saw on their journeys. Allow participants to choose the types of drawing utensils that they will use. Indicate that black and white drawings are just as acceptable as color.

d. Allow the use of words in the picture. Acknowledge that some participant's "pictures in their mind" will be words. The use of words is acceptable, but encourage participants to use picture representations of words when possible.

e. If the site of this meeting is conducive to having participants leave the room and find some private space, encourage them to do that. Ask participants to take a few minutes to reflect on their journey before they begin drawing.

6. Invite the participants to share their visions with each other, emphasizing the common themes of creating a successful and useful work group, serving customers, serving themselves, and personal values about work and achievement.

Introduce some simple ground rules for this part of the activity:

✓ There is no right or wrong when it comes to personal visions.

✓ Do not laugh or otherwise make fun of someone else's vision.

✓ Look for the commonality among the visions, but don't disregard the uncommon.

A word about positive reinforcement: Be very conscious of giving equal positive reinforcement to all participants. Whatever you do, whether it is clapping after each presentation, or saying thank you, or praising the vision, be consistent. Do the same for everyone.

7. Conclude the activity using one of the following:

✓ If this activity is the first of a series of team-building or relationship-building activities for a new team or work group, emphasize how participants will use their personal visions at the next meeting. Explain what the next steps will be.

✓ If increased unity is one of the reasons for conducting this activity, have participants create a large picture of all the visions (by taping them together like a quilt or collage) under the heading "Our Visions." The team leader should be responsible for bringing this picture to every subsequent meeting and/or displaying it in the work area.

✓ If this activity is a stand-alone session, talk about how participants might use their visions in their personal and professional lives. Consider using some material about "creative tension" from Peter Senge's *The Fifth Discipline.**

---

*Peter Senge, *The Fifth Discipline: The Art and Practice of the Learning Orgnization*, Garden City, NY: Doubleday, 1990, p. 150.

Variations:

1. Have participants write what they saw during their visualization instead of drawing a picture. Another variation is to have them write a 30-second radio spot advertising their preferred futures.

2. Increase the time allotted and have participants combine their personal visions into a group or shared vision. The finished product would be one pictorial representation of the "preferred workplace."

Vision

A vision can also be referred to as a "vision of greatness."[*] It is the way we want our future to be. It is something that is good for the individual, good for the department, and good for the company.

Visions are both "strategic and lofty"[†]—strategic in that they focus on how we contribute to the organization and lofty because they can "capture our imagination and engage our spirit."[‡]

Personal Vision

A personal vision comes from deep inside us, it is usually close to our heart and has deep personal meaning. It is a reflection of the values that are most important to us. Personal visions can be multifaceted, including material, personal, and service desires.

Here is an example of a personal vision for life outside work: freedom, a nice place to live, being true to yourself, and making a contribution to society.

Personal visions that relate to work should include ideas on creating a successful and useful work group, serving customers, and serving ourselves and should reflect personal values about work and achievement.

[*]Peter Block, *The Empowered Manager*, San Francisco: Jossey-Bass, 1987, p. 102.
[†]Ibid.
[‡]Ibid.

Read the text slowly so that participants have time to create images in their mind.

To help us create our personal visions of our life at work, we are going to make a journey into the future. You can take a plane, a train, a hang glider, any mode of transportation that you like. Try to visualize this mode of transportation and see yourself climbing aboard. As we fly or ride, we are riding above or through a beautiful forest. The sun is shining, the birds are singing. Slowly the forest fades into a populated area, and we arrive at [*insert your workplace name here*]. We fly or ride right into the building and somehow find our way to [*insert your work area, department, company here*]. The time is three years from now. We are here to observe what [*insert work group name here*] is like. Remember that visions are not practical—they are idealistic and almost spiritual. Visions are our desired future.

What do you see happening? Where are you? Where are your work colleagues? How are you working with your customers? How are you treating them, and how are they treating you? How are you working with the other people in your work group? How are you treating each other? How are you spending your time? What do meetings look like? What is the nature of your projects?

It is time to leave, and as we do so, we turn and take one last look at our desired, idealistic, spiritual future. We fly or ride away from [*insert your workplace name here*] into the beautiful, sunny forest. The sun is still shining and the birds are still singing. Slowly the surroundings become familiar. You are coming back in time to the present, to this neighborhood, to this building, to this room. You climb down from your chosen mode of transportation and slowly make your way back to your chair. You still see flashes of pictures from your journey in time. Take a minute to look at them, and when you are ready, open your eyes.

REFERENCES

Block, Peter. 1987. *The Empowered Manager.* San Francisco: Jossey-Bass.
Senge, Peter. 1990. *The Fifth Discipline: The Art and Practice of the Learning Organization.* Garden City, NY: Doubleday.

CLIMBING THE STEPS: HOW EMPOWERED IS YOUR TEAM?

Gary Topchik

Gary S. Topchik *is president of Silver Star Enterprises (1659 Bel Air Road, Suite A, Los Angeles, CA 90077, 1-800-471-8489, Gsilstar@aol.com), a training and organizational development consulting firm. From 1988 to 1991, Gary was chair of the New York Organizational Development Network, and in 1991 he was named the external consultant of the year by the Training Directors' Forum. Gary also teaches in the business and management department at the University of California at Los Angeles.*

Overview   This activity gives team members a reading on the level of empowerment of their own teams. It also provides an opportunity to discuss how much empowerment they desire. You can use this activity at any team gathering or during a team-building workshop where several teams have gathered.

Suggested Time   45 minutes

Materials Needed   Form A (How Empowered Is Our Team?)

Procedure   1. Ask participants to define an "empowered" team. Sample answers could include the following:

✓ Work is designed to give the team ownership of a service or product.

✓ The team plans, controls, and improves its own work processes.

✓ The team sets its own goals (in alignment with organizational goals) and measures the results of its own work.

✓ The team takes responsibility for the quality of its services or products.

✓ Members have the communication, listening, problem-solving, and consensus-building skills that make for effective teamwork.

Record the answers and ask if there are benefits to an organization of having teams with these skills and characteristics. Note their responses.

2. Distribute Form A and ask participants to review it. Ask each team member to find the step that best describes his or her current team and mark it with an X. Also, ask each of them to identify where he or she would want their team to be and mark it with a Y.

3. Invite team members to compare responses with one another.

4. If their perceptions are similar, immediately invite them to discuss the step of empowerment to which they would like to climb. Suggest that they brainstorm ways to get there, including ways to convince senior management to entrust them with greater empowerment.

5. If their perceptions are dissimilar, invite team members to discuss the reasons behind their assessments. Once reasons are given, check to see if differences in opinion still exist. If not, have the team now discuss the step of empowerment to which they would like to climb. If differences remain, urge the team to take more time to discuss its current level of empowerment. Suggest that a consensus is not required, but it is important to be clear of the different perceptions in the team.

6. *(optional)* Lead a discussion about the following questions:
   ✓ Why would team leaders or managers not want their teams to be at a high level of empowerment (fear of loss of control, lack of trust)?
   ✓ Why would some team members or entire teams not want to be empowered (fear of working on own, lack of confidence)?

_____ **Step 1** *Direct supervision and no decision making.* Our team is told exactly what to do by supervisors. We do not participate in any decision making. Very close and directive supervision is required.

_____ **Step 2** *Team input but no decisions.* Our team is asked for input, but supervisors still make decisions.

_____ **Step 3** *Team decides, but needs approval to act.* We advise and act. Our team tells the supervisor or manager before doing anything. The team is expected to know what to do, but is not encouraged to do it unless it is first approved.

_____ **Step 4** *Team decides, acts, and then tells supervision or managers.* Our team acts, then advises. We do what we think is right and then tell management.

_____ **Step 5** *Team acts on its own without telling management.* Our team acts on its own without informing.

_____ **Step 6** *Team acts and advises management on next steps.* Our team advises management about what can be done after the decision or action has already taken place.

_____ **Step 7** *Team acts completely autonomously on behalf of the company.* Our team is acting on behalf of the company, not just for an individual organization or department.

16

FROM CONTEST TO PARTNERSHIP: REDUCING CONFLICT IN YOUR ORGANIZATION

Sandy Rice, Rebecca Lane, and Kathleen Williams

Sandy Rice *is training manager for The Center for Health Training (421 E. 6th St., Ste. B, Austin TX 78701, 512-474-2166), a regional training center serving family planning and other public health providers in Texas, Louisiana, New Mexico, Arkansas, and Oklahoma.* **Rebecca Lane,** *Ph.D., is president of Compeer, Inc. (Rte. 1, Box 21, Spicewood, TX 78669, 512-264-2172), a private consulting and development company specializing in work with public health or nonprofit organizations.* **Kathleen Williams** *is training manager, Compeer, Inc. (Rte. 1, Box 21, Spicewood, TX 78669, 512-264-2172).*

Overview This activity helps to set the stage for training on specific strategies of organizational conflict resolution that emphasize a collaborative approach. Participants can explore the impact that metaphors and language have on their experiences of conflict and can physically experience a shift from seeing conflict as a *contest* to that of a *partnership*. By making this shift, they can move toward seeking win–win resolutions of conflict situations in their own organizational settings.

Suggested Time 30 minutes

Materials Needed Easel, pad, markers

Procedure 1. Briefly discuss the importance and impact of metaphors on our lives. Emphasize that metaphors often shape the way that we think and feel about people individually and in groups and about the issues of our day. Metaphors structure our reality and therefore determine the possibilities of our actions and attitudes.

2. Point out that one of the most common metaphors in our culture is the metaphor of *war.* We talk about the *battle of the sexes,* the *war on drugs,* and the *war on poverty.*

3. Ask the participants to consider how the *war* metaphor affects the way that they think about and experience an argument. Pose this

question: *What are some of the things we say before, during, and after arguments that make it sound like an experience of war or battle?*

4. List their responses on a flip chart. The list might include the following:

   ✓ He attacked every point in my argument.

   ✓ She shot down all my suggestions.

   ✓ My points were right on target.

   ✓ If you use that strategy, you'll be wiped out.

   ✓ I'll never win an argument with the boss.

   ✓ I annihilated their presentation.

5. Next, pose this question: *What would happen if we changed the metaphor "argument as war" to "argument as dance"? How would we then describe arguing?*

   Present some of the following list and invite other possibilities.

   ✓ We waltzed around the issue.

   ✓ She tripped over every point in my argument.

   ✓ He couldn't get the rhythm of my suggestions.

   ✓ I can't find the music to go with her choreography.

   ✓ If you try that step, you'll fall down.

6. Suggest that the *war* metaphor implies winning, destroying the opponent, and killing. By comparison, the *dance* metaphor recognizes common goals and the need to develop creative solutions. The former suggests *contest*; the latter suggests *partnership*.

7. Tell participants that you would like them to now experience this shift from *contest* to *partnership* physically as well as intellectually.

8. Have participants stand and get into pairs, facing each other. (Allow any participants with physical limitations to excuse themselves.) Ask one person in each pair to volunteer to get on his or her knees. Explain that the task of the standing person is to push the kneeling person down. The kneeler, arms hanging, is to resist. Instruct standing participants to be gentle and not hurt their partner, but to be firm. Give them 2 minutes for this experience. Encourage standing people to continually push down their partners—several times, if possible.

9. Next, instruct each pair to try again, the same person pushing and the same person resisting, but this time the kneeler should clasp the pusher's elbows. Again, give 2 minutes.

10. Ask, *How was it different this time?* (*Note:* Far less resistance is needed to stay upright. People report feeling more "in control.")

11. Point out that the key element is *reaching out—extending*. By working with "the opposition," a great deal more is accomplished than by simply fighting back.

12. Ask a volunteer to come up to the front. Have that person face you with hands raised and palms facing you. Place your palms against that person's palms and push gently toward her or him. The person will (probably) push back. Ask the group, *What if I suddenly join the other person?* (Demonstrate. It throws the other person off balance.)

13. Emphasize that it only takes one person in an argument to move from his or her initial position. In an argument, we typically get into "Yes, you are!"–"No I'm not!" positions. We can change this to "I see your point" or "Thanks for telling me." This has the effect of "disarming" our "opponent" and buys us time both to reflect and reach a new perspective.

14. Divide participants into subgroups of four or five. Ask them to relate these experiences in going from contest to partnership to the conflicts existing within their own organizations and workplaces. Instruct each group to come up with two to three work-related examples in which this transition might be made.

15. Reconvene the whole group and exchange examples. Discuss the possibilities of reducing organizational conflict with win–win approaches.

ASSESSMENT INSTRUMENTS

In this section of *The 1996 McGraw-Hill Team and Organization Development Sourcebook*, you will find seven assessment instruments. With these instruments, you will be able to assess:

✓ Organizational motivation.

✓ Customer service practices.

✓ Team functioning.

✓ Organizational results.

The instruments are designed both to evaluate team/organizational performance and to suggest areas for improvements. Most are not for research purposes. Instead, they are intended to build awareness, provide feedback about your own specific situation, and promote group reflection.

In selecting instruments for publication, a premium was placed on questionnaires or survey forms that are easy to understand and quick to complete. Preceding each instrument is an overview that contains the key questions to be assessed. The instruments themselves are on separate pages to make reproduction more convenient. All of the instruments are scorable and contain guidelines for scoring interpretation. Some include questions for followup discussion.

These instruments are ideal to utilize as activities in training programs, organizational retreats, or team meetings. Have participants complete the instruments prior to the session. Then, summarize the results and open them up to team discussion.

If you choose this option, be sure to state the process clearly to respondents. You might want to use the following text:

> *We are planning to get together soon to identify issues that need to be worked through in order to maximize our future effectivenss. An excellent way to begin doing some of this work is to collect information through a questionnaire and to feed back that information for group discussion.*
>
> *I would like you to join with your colleagues in filling out the attached questionnaire. Your honest responses will enable the team to have a clear view of itself.*
>
> *Your participation will be totally anonymous. My job will be to summarize the results and report them to the team for group reaction.*

You can also share the instruments with others in your organization who might find them useful for their own purposes. In some cases, merely reading through the questions is a valuable exercise in self- and group reflection.

HOW MOTIVATING IS YOUR ORGANIZATION?

Dean Spitzer

Dean R. Spitzer, *Ph.D., is president of Dean R. Spitzer & Associates, Inc. (5150 S. Florida Avenue, Suite 316, Lakeland, Florida 33813, 941-648-2754), a firm specializing in enhancing organizational motivation. He is a former vice-president of the National Society for Performance & Instruction (NSPI), the author of numerous publications, and a contributor to the* **Handbook of Human Performance Technology.** *Dr. Spitzer's latest book is* **SuperMotivation: A Blueprint for Energizing Your Organization from Top to Bottom** *(AMACOM Books, 1995).*

OVERVIEW

Did you ever wonder how to measure *organizational* motivation (in contrast to *personal* motivation)? *The Motivated Organization Survey* is an easily administered self-reporting instrument that provides a valid and reliable method for assessing motivation in any organization, department, or work unit. It consists of 60 items drawn from the characteristics of high-motivation organizations (Spitzer, *SuperMotivation*, AMACOM, 1995). When taken together, the items that comprise the survey provide a kind of vision, or operational definition, of the highly motivated organization.

You can use this survey to assess the motivational climate in your organization, to monitor motivational development and change, or as a component in supervisory and management training to discuss the characteristics of motivated organizations.

THE MOTIVATED ORGANIZATION SURVEY

In the space to the right of each statement, place a number (from 1 to 5) indicating *how true* the statement is *about your organization,* using the following rating scale:

1 = not true at all
2 = true to a small extent
3 = true to some extent
4 = mostly true
5 = completely true

1. Employees in this organization are energetic and enthusiastic. _____

2. Employees are highly productive. _____

3. Employees have positive and optimistic attitudes. _____

4. There is little or no wasted effort. _____

5. This organization is highly customer-focused. _____

6. Unsafe conditions are identified and promptly corrected. _____

7. Employees are made to feel like true business partners. _____

8. Employees have a strong sense of organizational identity. _____

9. Employees are very careful in how they use the organization's resources. _____

10. Employees have a clear understanding of the organization's mission, vision, and values. _____

11. Employee input into organizational strategic planning is solicited and used. _____

12. Employees are encouraged to make significant choices and decisions about their work. _____

13. Employees are involved in making key production decisions. _____

14. Employees are empowered to improve work methods. _____

15. Employees are encouraged to work closely with their internal customers and suppliers. _____

16. There is a no-fault approach to problem solving in this organization. _____

17. A concerted effort is made to identify and use the full range of abilities that employees bring to work. _____

18. Employees are challenged to strive for ambitious goals. _____

19. Obstacles to effective employee performance are promptly identified and eliminated. _____

20. Personnel decisions are perceived to be fair and consistent. _____

21. There are few, if any, unnecessary policies and rules. _____

22. Effective communication is a high organizational priority. _____

23. Employees throughout this organization are well informed. _____

24. Management explains to employees the rationale behind all important decisions. _____

25. There is frequent communication between employees and management. _____

26. Senior managers regularly visit employees' work areas. _____

27. No secrets are kept from employees. _____

28. Meetings are well led and highly productive. _____

29. Company publications are informative and helpful. _____

30. Management is highly responsive to employees' needs and concerns. _____

31. Employees feel that management has their best interests at heart. _____

32. When labor–management conflicts arise, they are promptly and constructively resolved. _____

33. Management is quick to take personal responsibility for its mistakes. _____

34. Employees are encouraged to assume leadership responsibilities. _____

35. Employees receive a great deal of encouragement and recognition. _____

36. Outstanding performance is always recognized. _____

37. Both individual and team performance is appropriately rewarded. _____

38. Poor performance is never rewarded. _____

39. Creativity is encouraged and rewarded. _____

40. Employees consider their pay to be fair and equitable. _____

41. Employees are willing to pay part of the cost of their benefits. _____

42. Employees feel that their ideas and suggestions are genuinely welcomed by management. _____

43. Employees' suggestions receive prompt and constructive responses. _____

44. Everyone in the organization is committed to continuous improvement. _____

45. There are no barriers between departments or units. _____

46. There is a high level of trust between workers and management. _____

47. There is excellent teamwork throughout the organization. _____

48. There is a high level of interdepartmental communication and cooperation throughout the organization. _____

49. Management views problems as opportunities for improvement, rather than as obstacles to success. _____

50. Learning is a high priority in this organization. _____

51. Employees are encouraged to learn from each other. _____

52. There is consistent follow-up after training. _____

53. Employees are involved in making training decisions. _____

54. Employees are involved in determining performance requirements, measures, and standards. _____

55. Employees view performance evaluation as a positive development process. _____

56. Self-evaluation and peer evaluation are integral components of performance appraisal. _____

57. Discipline is perceived to be fair. _____

58. Employees consistently give extra effort. _____

59. Tardiness, absenteeism, and turnover rates are extremely low. _____

60. Employees are excited about working in this organization. _____

Total score (add all item responses): _____

Percentage score (divide by 300): _____ %

Add all your responses to determine your total score. (If surveys were completed by a group, compute a mean score for each item.) A perfect score would be 300 (based on a maximum response of 5 for each of the 60 items on the survey). When you divide your total score by 300, you will obtain an overall percentage score. The higher the percentage score, the higher the perceived level of organizational motivation.

Here are some guidelines for helping you interpret your organization's percentage score:

90%–100%	Congratulations! Your organization has already attained high-motivation status.
80%–89%	Your organization is well on its way to high motivation.
70%–79%	Your organization has some of the characteristics of a high-motivation organization.
60%–69%	Your organization has a slightly above average* motivational climate.
50%–59%	Your organization has an average* motivational climate.
Below 50%	Your organization has a below average* motivational climate.

*Based on national norms for this survey.

18

ARE YOU HELPING TO CREATE LOYAL CUSTOMERS?

Barbara Glanz

Barbara Glanz, *president of Barbara Glanz Communications, Inc. (4047 Howard Avenue, Western Springs, IL 60558, 708-246-8594), is an internationally known professional speaker and consultant. She is the author of* **The Creative Communicator—399 Tools to Communicate Commitment without Boring People to Death!** *(Irwin, 1993),* **Building Customer Loyalty—How YOU Can Help Keep Customers Returning** *(Irwin, 1994), and* **C.A.R.E. Packages for the Workplace: Activities to Regenerate Spirit, Hope, and Caring,** *to be published by McGraw-Hill.*

OVERVIEW

Customer focus is the key to survival for organizations today. Not only must companies acquire new customers, but more importantly, they must keep the old ones. Research shows that it costs five times as much to acquire a new customer as it does to retain an existing customer. It becomes essential, then, for a company to understand which service attributes create customer loyalty and to take a hard look at where an organization is spending the bulk of its time, money, and energy—on creating loyal customers or on acquiring new ones. This instrument addresses the need to create customer loyalty at the one-on-one interaction level with a customer, thus giving each employee a feeling of participation and a sense of mission that he or she *can* make a difference. It is only through specific, memorable behaviors that individuals create customer loyalty.

The *Building Customer Loyalty Self-assessment* focuses on the specific behaviors that research has shown create loyal customers. These behaviors are observable and measurable, and they become guidelines for every employee in his or her behavior toward customers, both internal and external. If organizations today want to stay in business, they must do more than simply acquire new customers. They must treat their established customers in such a way that they *want* to do more business with the organization. Assessing how well you are already building customer loyalty is the first step in taking individual responsibility for doing just that.

BUILDING CUSTOMER LOYALTY SELF-ASSESSMENT*

Use this self-assessment to see how your actions are contributing toward building a loyal customer base. Check the answer that most often describes your behavior toward your direct customers.

Almost Always	Sometimes	Almost Never	
_____	_____	_____	**1.** I know my products well, and I always try to teach my customer a little more about my organization's products or services.
_____	_____	_____	**2.** I offer my customers options and alternatives so that they may make a wise decision.
_____	_____	_____	**3.** I explain all information, especially answers to their concerns and questions, carefully, fully, and respectfully.
_____	_____	_____	**4.** I do things for my customers even when it is not my job to do them.
_____	_____	_____	**5.** I take personal responsibility to solve a customer's problem. I don't simply dump it on someone else.
_____	_____	_____	**6.** I routinely follow up with several of my customers each week to see if they are happy with our products or services.
_____	_____	_____	**7.** I learn my customers' names whenever possible, and I use their names at least once in a conversation.
_____	_____	_____	**8.** I remember customers' names when they return to my place of work.

*This self-assessment instrument is excerpted with permission from Barbara Glanz, *Building Customer Loyalty—How YOU Can Help Keep Customers Returning*, Irwin Professional Publishing, Burr Ridge, IL, 1994.

_____ _____ _____ **9.** I work at noticing something special about each person or listening for personal information that they might share.

_____ _____ _____ **10.** I am willing to bend the rules for my customers.

_____ _____ _____ **11.** I am willing to give up some personal time (breaks, lunchtime, at the end of my shift) when the customer needs it.

_____ _____ _____ **12.** I often do something extra to surprise and please my customer.

_____ _____ _____ **13.** I treat every customer as if he or she were my friend or neighbor, and I try to put myself in his or her shoes.

_____ _____ _____ **14.** I take a sincere personal interest in my customers—their families, their jobs, their needs. I work hard at remembering special things about them, and I inquire about these things when I talk with them again.

_____ _____ _____ **15.** I _really_ listen to my customer's needs and feelings; then I _act_ on what I hear.

_____ _____ _____ **16.** When either I or my organization makes a mistake, I apologize sincerely to the customer, and I do my very best to fix it. Then I do something extra.

_____ _____ _____ **17.** I often make suggestions of other things we can do to help the customer. If I or my organization cannot, with creative thinking, solve the customer's problem, I will recommend another source, perhaps even a competitor.

_____ _____ _____ **18.** I trust my customers and always assume that their intentions are honest.

Almost Always	Sometimes	Almost Never	
_____	_____	_____	**19.** I always express my thanks and appreciation for choosing our organization when I help a customer.
_____	_____	_____	**20.** I always treat the customer with respect, making the customer feel more important than me or my organization.
_____	_____	_____	**21.** I stay calm and respectful even with a customer who is arguing with me.
_____	_____	_____	**22.** I empathize with the customer's concerns, even if I do not agree with them. I use listening skills to acknowledge his or her feelings and show the customer that I care.
_____	_____	_____	**23.** Even when the customer is not there, I do what is best for *them*, not what is easiest or fastest for me.
_____	_____	_____	**24.** I am creative in thinking of ways that I can add my personal signature to my work and delight my customers.
_____	_____	_____	**25.** I follow through as quickly as possible when I make a promise to a customer. This includes returning phone calls within 24 hours.
_____	_____	_____	**26.** I ask clear, appropriate questions to clarify or gather the additional information that I need to be sure I fully understand a customer's situation.
_____	_____	_____	**27.** Even in the midst of confusion, long lines, phones ringing, emergencies, and constant other interruptions, I stay calm and treat each customer with friendliness, courtesy, and patience.
_____	_____	_____	**28.** I smile a lot and share how much I enjoy my job and my customers.

Look through your responses and add up the number of times that you put check marks in each column. If the majority of your marks are in the "Almost Always," column, then you are already exhibiting the kinds of behaviors that build strong customer loyalty. If the majority of your marks are in the "Sometimes" or "Almost Never" columns, read through the following list of questions and reflect on how you can individually make a difference in building a loyal customer base for your organization.

1. Do these behaviors reflect the way *you* would like to be treated as a customer?

2. Which behaviors do you feel you need to work on the most?

3. What reminders, information, or skills might help you to be more consistent in using these behaviors?

4. Which behaviors are you already using consistently with your customers?

5. How did you learn to use these behaviors?

6. Can you think of any other specific behaviors that have helped *you* to become a loyal customer?

WHAT ARE YOUR TEAM'S NEEDS?

Phil Lohr and Patricia Steege

Phil Lohr *and* **Patricia Steege** *work as internal management development/organization development consultants for Lockheed Martin's Enterprise Information Systems (EIS) Company, Bldg. 10, Room 1284D, PO Box 8048, Philadelphia, PA 19101. Phil (610-364-5338, philip.j. lohr@den.mmc.com) authored the 1993 Best Practitioner Paper entitled "Empowering the Knowledge Worker: Strategies, Instruments, and Processes" at the International Conference on Self-managed Work Teams. Prior to switching to the MD/OD profession, Phil was a program manager and software systems developer. Phil is also a master practitioner of neuro linguistic and time line therapy. Tricia (610-354-5739, tricia.steege@den.mmc.com) specializes in team and leadership development.*

OVERVIEW

Teams go through natural growth and development stages as their members form, storm, norm and perform. Properly diagnosing the developmental stage and associated needs of a team allows you to make immediate interventions to spur the team in its growth.

Use the *Team Needs Assessment* that follows to diagnose a team's development and compare the information to that gained through interviewing individuals for feedback. The resulting combination of information will help you to address training and leadership issues with teams, units, task groups or any other organizational group with whom you work.

TEAM NEEDS ASSESSMENT

Answer each question as it relates to your team or task group situation.

For the purpose of this assessment, the term *team* can represent a work team at any stage of development, an individual contributor, a unit, a task group, or any other organizational structure in which work is accomplished.

Use the following guide for this assessment.

How important to team's success?	*Team or members exhibit behaviors*
1 = not important to success of team	1 = not at all
2 = somewhat important; could enhance success	2 = to a small degree
3 = important; makes success more likely	3 = to a moderate degree
4 = very important; success difficult without it	4 = yes, with room to improve
5 = critical to success of team	5 = totally, completely

How Important Is It?	← Circle one number in each column →	*How Much Do We Do It?*
1 2 3 4 5	**1.** Team operates with a common understanding of vision and objectives.	1 2 3 4 5
1 2 3 4 5	**2.** Team uses specific, measurable, and time-dimensioned goals (for example, reduce defects per transaction by 30% by March 1997).	1 2 3 4 5
1 2 3 4 5	**3.** Team uses feedback loops with its customers to measure its performance.	1 2 3 4 5
1 2 3 4 5	**4.** Team members can accurately describe the roles and responsibilities of all other members.	1 2 3 4 5
1 2 3 4 5	**5.** Team has negotiated its task responsibilities and decision authority levels with management (for example, hiring, vacation scheduling, and training plan).	1 2 3 4 5

How Important Is It?	← Circle one number in each column →	How Much Do We Do It?
1 2 3 4 5	**6.** Team makes consensus decisions with buy-in from all members.	1 2 3 4 5
1 2 3 4 5	**7.** Team follows established guidelines for its operations (for example, meeting management and task assignments).	1 2 3 4 5
1 2 3 4 5	**8.** Team follows and references established norms for member behavior (that is, a team code of conduct).	1 2 3 4 5
1 2 3 4 5	**9.** Team members hold each other accountable, with known consequences, for individual performance and adherence to team guidelines.	1 2 3 4 5
1 2 3 4 5	**10.** Team holds regular, effective meetings with good facilitation.	1 2 3 4 5
1 2 3 4 5	**11.** Team members effectively listen to each other.	1 2 3 4 5
1 2 3 4 5	**12.** Team members effectively give and receive feedback (both positive and negative).	1 2 3 4 5
1 2 3 4 5	**13.** Members effectively manage conflict inside and outside of group settings.	1 2 3 4 5
1 2 3 4 5	**14.** Belief and culture differences are valued when viewing behaviors and decisions in the work setting.	1 2 3 4 5
1 2 3 4 5	**15.** Members recognize each others' behavioral style differences and leverage them to mutual advantage.	1 2 3 4 5
1 2 3 4 5	**16.** Team uses appropriate tools and techniques to make group decisions (for example, a problem selection matrix).	1 2 3 4 5

How Important Is It?	← Circle one number in each column →	How Much Do We Do It?
1 2 3 4 5	**17.** Team analyzes its work process using appropriate tools (for example, process mapping).	1 2 3 4 5
1 2 3 4 5	**18.** Team uses program management skills to achieve its objectives (for example, task prioritization and scheduling).	1 2 3 4 5
1 2 3 4 5	**19.** Team assesses its impact within the larger organization.	1 2 3 4 5
1 2 3 4 5	**20.** Team members plan and use their time effectively.	1 2 3 4 5
1 2 3 4 5	**21.** Team members identify symptoms of stress and take appropriate action when necessary.	1 2 3 4 5
1 2 3 4 5	**22.** Team members can articulate their career objectives and are working toward them.	1 2 3 4 5

SCORING THE TEAM NEEDS ASSESSMENT

1. To obtain the outcome value, multiply the value of the left-hand column by the inverse value of the right-hand column response. For example, if the respondent indicates that a common understanding among the team is important and rates it with a 4 (left-hand column value), but rates how much it is being done with a 2, multiply 4 × 4 (inverse value of 2) to receive an outcome value of 16. If the right-hand column rates a 5, you would multiply 4 × 1 (the inverse value of 5) to receive an outcome value of 4.

   The inverse value represents the need or *gap*. As in the preceding example, if the group has indicated that the importance is a 5 and has also indicated that it is not being done by rating it a 1, this is the greatest need that is not being met. By multiplying the left-hand column by the inverse value of the right-hand column, the number will be greatest that shows the greatest need. A rating of 3 remains a 3.

2. For each question, calculate its total average value by adding all the outcome values and dividing the total by the number of respondents. For example, if 10 individuals participated and the total sum of the outcome values of question 1 is 110, the average value is 11 (110/10).

3. To determine the entire survey median value, add the average values of all the questions (as calculated in step 2) and divide by the total number of respondents. Using a spreadsheet tool, plot a chart depicting the average values for each question.

INTERPRETING THE TEAM NEEDS ASSESSMENT

1. The median value will indicate the overall health of the group on a scale of 1 to 25. A relatively higher median score (15 and above) indicates that the group is most likely highly dysfunctional and needs several interventions, whereas a lower median score (9 or below) indicates that the group believes it is functioning fairly effectively.

2. Scores falling farthest above the median value point indicate the greatest perceived needs by the team. Scores falling farthest below the median value point indicate that the team did not currently perceive a need although it possibly could become a need at a later date. Because the questions are grouped in team development stages, it is likely that the score results will be in grouped order. For example, if a group of scores falls highest in questions 1 through 9, this indicates that the group is in its *forming* stages. Likewise, scores will be highest for questions 17 through 22 when a group is in its *performing* stage.

SHOULD YOUR TEAM BE REVITALIZED?

Wayne Pace and Douglas McGregor

R. Wayne Pace, *Ph.D., is professor of organizational behavior, Marriott School of Management, Brigham Young University. Dr. Pace has been president of the Academy of Human Resource Development, the International Communication Association , and the Western States Communication Association. He is the author of 15 books and dozens of articles, monographs, and research reports on organizational behavior and communication. Dr. Pace may be contacted about issues of work-force revitalization at 440 East 2320 North, Provo, Utah 84604, 801-374-2870.* **Douglas R. McGregor** *is senior organizational performance technologist, Control Systems Division, Parker Bertea Aerospace, a division of Parker Hannifin Corporation. Doug may be contacted about issues of revitalization at 515 15th street, Ogden, Utah 84404, 801-392-4002.*

OVERVIEW

The spirit, enthusiasm, vigor, intensity, and persistence with which team members do their work is, nowadays, the competitive edge among organizations. Sheer technical talent is not enough. *Time* magazine recognized this shift in competitiveness in 1989 when it ran the cover story under the question, "Where Did the Gung Ho Go?" Janice Castro, the writer, pointed out the critical drop in employee work intensity and spirit and a serious underlying decline in commitment and productivity.

The *Team Vitality Inventory* is an instrument that provides a look at the underlying factors that engender "gung ho" or vitality in teams.

Both research and the experience of living in organizations indicate that vitality at work is revealed by four basic perceptions:

1. How well employees' expectations are met by the organization

2. What employees think their opportunities are in the organization

3. How employees feel about the amount of fulfillment they derive from working in the organization

4. What perceptions employees have of how well they are performing in the organization

98

Expectations

Most of us started working with the anticipation and hope that what we were doing would lead to continued advances in income, position, status, responsibility, or other benefits. Reid and Evans (1983) have observed, for example, that "people begin their careers hopeful that they will be continually promoted" (p. 86). As we live and work in organizations, promises are both kept and not kept, leading to met and upset expectations. Expectations represent what people think will happen to them. Promises are the assurances that lead to expectations. When we are assured that something will happen, we are led to expect it to happen. Thus, one major factor that reveals or reflects work vitality is a person's reactions to how well his or her expectations have been met by the organization for which the person works.

Fulfillment

One reason why unmet expectations lead to such negative consequences for employees is the keen sense that failed expectations is a sign of an unfulfilled life. A fulfilled life is one in which the individual is able to do things in unique and creative ways.

Opportunity

Opportunity is the perception that we are able to advance or move ahead in the organization. Opportunity may be the most powerful of the four perceptions since it has such potentially devastating consequences when not present. For opportunity to exist, conditions must be favorable for the attainment of a goal. Thus, if you are employed in an organization where few or no conditions are favorable to achieving that goal, we may say that you lack opportunity.

Performance

Perceptions of performance have to do with employees' views of how well they can do their jobs in the organization. Perceptions are concerned less with actual performance and more with one's image of performance. Bandura (1977) uses the term "self-efficacy" to describe one's belief that one is able to execute a specific task successfully or competently in order to achieve a certain outcome.

Perceptions of performance, as encompassed in the concept of self-efficacy, are considered some of the most influential factors on the behavior of people in everyday situations, especially at work. A growing body of evidence suggests that people's perception of their ability to perform is the most critical factor in achievement. Since perceptions of performance are judgments about our capabilities to accomplish some goal, these perceptions are intimately connected with vitality in our work lives.

These four positive perceptions—performance (P), opportunity (O), fulfillment (F), and expectations (E), abbreviated POFE—combine to create an image or mindset that produces vitality at work. The vigor with which teams function is affected by the work perceptions of team members.

TEAM VITALITY INVENTORY

The *Team Vitality Inventory* provides a measure of the strength of your team in four critical areas. Thus, think of your team as a whole as you complete the inventory.

1. Respond to all questions as honestly and frankly as you possibly can. In no way will your identity be associated with your responses nor will your responses be used to jeopardize or compromise your position on the team.

2. Unless the wording of a particular item specifically indicates otherwise, mark your answers in terms of the team in which you work.

3. Indicate your response to each item by filling in the appropriate space on the answer sheet. Do not omit any items.

4. Do not attempt an intensive word analysis of the statements. Your responses should reflect your own judgment, not those of anyone else. There are no right or wrong answers.

Thank you very much for completing this inventory.

Instructions: On the following answer sheet, circle the numerical rating that corresponds with the way that you feel about the team in which you are currently working. Do not try to analyze the statements, but think about how you *feel* at this time. Read each statement, but answer as quickly as you can.

1. This team is recognized by all team members as being vital.

   Disagree   1   2   3   4   5   Agree

2. This team creates products and/or services that are of great value.

   Disagree   1   2   3   4   5   Agree

3. This team provides all members with opportunities to excel.

   Disagree   1   2   3   4   5   Agree

4. This team anticipates that its members will achieve their goals and aspirations.

   Disagree   1   2   3   4   5   Agree

5. This team encourages its members to do their work in unique and clever ways.

   Disagree   1   2   3   4   5   Agree

6. This team expects to surpass its former goals and accomplishments.

   Disagree   1   2   3   4   5   Agree

7. This team encourages all members to do their work at the highest levels of technical skill that they are capable of.

   Disagree   1   2   3   4   5   Agree

8. This team anticipates meeting the individual needs of its members.

   Disagree   1   2   3   4   5   Agree

9. Members of this team have committed themselves to pursuing its goals with vigor.

   Disagree   1   2   3   4   5   Agree

10. This team expects to find answers and challenge the status quo.

> Disagree   1   2   3   4   5   Agree

11. This team learns, grows, and develops from the work it does.

> Disagree   1   2   3   4   5   Agree

12. This team encourages its members to engage in various functional activities to achieve its goals.

> Disagree   1   2   3   4   5   Agree

13. This team supports values, has a great future vision, and mobilizes energy to solve problems.

> Disagree   1   2   3   4   5   Agree

14. This team encourages individual team members to improve their skills.

> Disagree   1   2   3   4   5   Agree

15. This team values individual and unique contributions from each member.

> Disagree   1   2   3   4   5   Agree

16. This team enjoys working together.

> Disagree   1   2   3   4   5   Agree

17. This team works so well that its members will be successful and rewarded for what they do.

> Disagree   1   2   3   4   5   Agree

18. This team gives responsibility to all members and allows them to share in supervising themselves.

> Disagree   1   2   3   4   5   Agree

19. This team believes in constantly fighting team decay and lost vitality.

> Disagree   1   2   3   4   5   Agree

20. This team prizes highly skilled team members.

> Disagree   1   2   3   4   5   Agree

SCORING FORM

Place the numerical rating that you gave to each of the 20 statements in the space next to it. Then sum the numbers to obtain a score for each of the four categories.

Vitality	Performance	Opportunity	Fulfillment	Expectations
1. _____	2. _____	3. _____	5. _____	4. _____
9. _____	7. _____	11. _____	15. _____	6. _____
13. _____	12. _____	14. _____	16. _____	8. _____
19. _____	20. _____	17. _____	18. _____	10. _____
Total:	Total:	Total:	Total:	Total:

Scores between 17 and 20 are considered high.

Scores between 13 and 16 are considered average.

Scores of 12 or below are considered low.

Sum the totals above to obtain a composite score.

Vitality =   _____

Performance =   _____

Opportunity =   _____

Fulfillment =   _____

Expectations =   _____

    Composite Score = _____

A composite score between 84 and 100 is considered high.

A composite score between 64 and 83 is considered average.

A composite score of 63 or below is considered low.

INTERPRETATION OF RESULTS

Overall Vitality Perceptions

When employees feel that they are unable to cope, when they are frustrated, overworked, disappointed, and confused, when they are unable to maintain their energy, enthusiasm, creativity and innovativeness, and when others notice a decline in their personal commitment, confidence, vision, and dedication at work, then we say that they have lost their vitality.

Managers and other employees who have lost their vitality are often referred to as peaked, on the shelf, over the hill, burned out, stomped on and passed over, or plateaued. These terms may seem pejorative, but their use implies strong feelings about the plight of managers, professionals, and other employees who have lost their vitality at work.

Low or average scores on vitality perceptions are clear signs that team members are experiencing feelings of lost vitality. The implication is that the team is being hindered from deriving adequate positive excitement from its work and from engaging in teamwork with enthusiasm and energy. This is a signal that the team is not performing as well as it could.

Performance Perceptions

Low or average scores on performance perceptions indicate that team members lack self-confidence in their ability to achieve their goals. For some reason, team members may have doubts about their abilities to accomplish their goals. When team members doubt that they have the ability to achieve their goals, they will most likely avoid doing what may be necessary to be successful.

Opportunity Perceptions

Low or average scores on opportunity perceptions indicate that team members feel that they are unable to move ahead in the organization. Lack of opportunity has been linked to five detrimental effects on behavior in organizations and teams: (1) reduction in the self-esteem of teams members, (2) lowered aspirations of team members, (3) reductions in levels of commitment of team members to the team and the organization, (4) an increase in negative comments about the team with a diversion of energy from tasks to gossip, and (5) increases in passive grumbling and some delight in seeing the team and the organization in trouble.

Low or average scores on fulfillment perceptions indicate that team members feel that they are unable to do their work in unique, individual, and original ways. Work that is unfulfilling is perceived as doing tasks that are not very important or don't seem to contribute to other things around the work area. Meaningless work puts a premium on shabby results, on slowdown, and on other ways to get the same pay with less work.

Expectations Perceptions

Low scores on expectations perceptions indicate that team members feel that the real or imagined promises on which they were counting have not been met as they would like. Expectations represent people's aspirations or what they would like to achieve. Promises are the assurances that our hopes and aspirations will be met. Some experts have suggested that failed expectations results in burnout. Lost vitality in a team is attributable in part to unmet expectations.

QUESTIONS FOR REFLECTION AND DISCUSSION

Instructions: Individually or as a team, review your scores on the Team Vitality Inventory and in writing or orally with other team members, answer the following questions:

1. To what extent do your average or composite scores on the entire TVI compare with how you feel about your team and how it functions?

2. Which of the subscores—V, P, O, F, or E—correlates with or matches most closely the overall, composite score on the TVI? Why?

3. On which of the four key perceptions—P, O, F, or E—were your subscores the lowest? Why?

4. Why do your perceptions of aspects of the workplace affect the amount of enthusiasm and energy you have to devote to teamwork?

5. What would your team like to have the company or organization in which you are working do to increase the vitality of your team?

6. To what extent would you agree with the following statement: "People must be working on what interests them, learning, growing, developing, and contributing. People today must understand the workplace as a whole, not just a piece of it." Explain your response.

7. To what extent is it possible to increase the vitality of teams in the workplace? Why? What could you do as a team to make your team a more vital unit?

REFERENCES

Abel, Kenneth Ross. 1971. Sensitivity to Workrole-Related Expectations and Perceived Promotability. Unpublished doctoral dissertation, University of California, Los Angeles, 1971.

Bandura, Albert. 1977. Self-efficacy: Toward a unifying theory of behavioral change. *Psychological Review*, 84, 191–215.

Boulding, Kenneth. 1956. *The Image*. Ann Arbor: University of Michigan Press.

Castro, Janice. 1989. Where did the gung ho go? *Time*, September 11, 52–54.

Drucker, Peter F. 1946. *Concept of the Corporation*. New York: John Day Co.

Kinlaw, Dennis C. 1988. What employees "see" is what organizations "get." *Management Solutions*, 33, 38–42.

Macleod, J. S. 1985 (Autumn). The work place as prison. *Employment Relations Today*, 215–218.

Miller, Donald B. 1977. *Personal Vitality*. Reading, MA: Addison-Wesley Publishing Co.

Pace, R. Wayne, and Dar-Yu Jaw. 1993. Organizational vitality: The key to productivity and quality improvement. *Journal of National Chengchi University*, 66, 385–395.

Reid, Robert D., and Michael R. Evans. 1988. The career plateau: What to do when a career bogs down. *Cornell Hotel and Restaurant Administration Quarterly*, 24, August, 83–91.

Yates, Ronald E. 1995. Downsizing moral: Morale needs a lift. *Chicago Tribune*, January, p. 1, business section.

HOW RESULTS-BASED ARE YOUR
HRD PROGRAMS?

Jack Phillips

Jack J. Phillips, *Ph.D., has served in several managerial and executive positions over 25 years including HRD manager and bank president. He serves on the graduate faculty at Middle Tennessee State University and provides consulting services in human resource accountability to a wide range of clients in 10 countries. Jack is a series editor for* **In Action: Case Studies,** *published by the American Society for Training and Development. He can be reached at PO Box 1969, Murfreesboro, Tennessee, 37133-1969, 615-896-7694.*

OVERVIEW

The instrument that follows, *The Human Resource Development Programs Assessment*, assesses the degree to which the HRD programs within your organization focus on results. Many organizations are deliberately making the shift away from an activity-based process to one that is characterized by a concern for results from programs during needs analysis, program development, and delivery. Members of your HRD staff, your HRD manager, and other managers within your organization can all benefit from this assessment instrument as an indicator of whether they are supporting a results-based HRD environment.

The Human Resource Development Programs Assessment has been used in the following ways:

✓ To assess the current status with a results-based HRD and to determine areas where additional improvement is needed

✓ As a yardstick for measuring improvement with the HRD staff (annual assessment)

✓ To compare divisions or plants in the same organization

✓ With line managers to stimulate discussion and dialogue to change the emphasis on HRD

✓ With top executives to gain their perspective and to stimulate dialogue for making changes in HRD

✓ To compare with standardized data (which are now available on 10 countries and can be obtained from the author)

HUMAN RESOURCE DEVELOPMENT PROGRAMS ASSESSMENT

Select the response that most accurately describes the current status of human resource programs within your organization. Please be candid.

1. HRD programs are
   a. Activity-oriented. (All supervisors attend the Performance Appraisal Workshop.)
   b. Individual results-based. (The participant will reduce his or her error rate by at least 20%.)
   c. Organizational results-based. (The cost of quality will decrease by 25%.)

2. The investment in HRD is measured primarily by
   a. Accident; there is no consistent measurement.
   b. Observations by management, reactions from participants.
   c. Dollar return through improved productivity, cost savings, or better quality.

3. The concern for the method of evaluation in the design and implementation of an HRD program occurs
   a. When the program is completed.
   b. When the program is developed, before it is conducted.
   c. Before the program is developed.

4. HRD efforts consist of
   a. Usually one-shot, seminar-type approaches.
   b. A full array of courses to meet individual needs.
   c. A variety of training and education programs implemented to bring about change in the organization.

5. Cost–benefit comparisons of HRD programs are
   a. Never developed.
   b. Occasionally developed.
   c. Frequently developed.

6. HRD programs, without some formal method of evaluation, are implemented
   a. Regularly.
   b. Seldom.
   c. Never.

7. The results of HRD programs are communicated
   a. When requested, to those who have a need to know.
   b. Occasionally, to members of management only.
   c.. Routinely, to a variety of selected target audiences.

8. The HRD staff involvement in evaluation consists of
   a. No specific responsibilities in evaluation, with no formal training in evaluation methods.
   b. Part of the staff having responsibilities for evaluation, with some formal training.
   c. All members of the staff having some responsibilities in evaluation, even if some are devoted full-time to the effort; all staff members have been trained in evaluation.

9. In an economic downturn the HRD function will
   a. Be the first to have its staff reduced.
   b. Be retained at the same staffing level.
   c. Go untouched in staff reductions and possibly be beefed up.

10. Budgeting for HRD is based on
    a. Last year's budget.
    b. Whatever the department head can "sell."
    c. A zero-based system.

11. HRD is funded through
    a. The training department budget.
    b. The administrative budget.
    c. Line operating budgets.

12. The principal group that must justify HRD expenditures is
    a. The training department.
    b. Various staff areas, including human resource.
    c. Line management.

13. Over the last two years, the HRD budget as a percent of operating expenses has
    a. Decreased.
    b. Remained stable.
    c. Increased.

14. The CEO interfaces with the manager responsible for HRD
    a. Never; it is a delegated responsibility.
    b. Occasionally, when someone recommends it.
    c. Frequently, to know what is going on.

15. The CEO's involvement in the implementation of HRD programs is

    a. Limited to sending invitations, extending congratulations, passing out certificates, and the like.

    b. Monitoring progress, opening and closing speeches, presentation on the outlook of the organization, and the like.

    c. Program participation to see what is covered, conducting major segments of the program, requiring key executives to be involved, and the like.

16. On the organization chart, the HRD manager

    a. Is more than two levels removed from the top executive.

    b. Is two levels below the top executive.

    c. Reports directly to the top executive.

17. Line management involvement in implementing HRD programs is

    a. Very minor; only HRD specialists conduct programs.

    b. Limited to a few specialists conducting programs in their area of expertise.

    c. Significant; on the average, over half of the programs are conducted by key line managers.

18. When an employee completes an HRD program and returns to the job, his or her supervisor usually

    a. Makes no reference to the program.

    b. Asks questions about the program and encourages the use of the material.

    c. Requires use of the program material and gives positive rewards when the material is used successfully.

19. When an employee attends an outside seminar, upon return he or she is required to

    a. Do nothing.

    b. Submit a report summarizing the program.

    c. Evaluate the seminar, outline plans for implementing the material covered, and estimate the value of the program.

20. With the present HRD organization and attitude toward results, the HRD function's impact on profit

    a. Can never be assessed accurately.

    b. Can be estimated, but probably at a significant cost.

    c. Can be estimated (or is being estimated) with little cost.

Score the assessment instrument as follows. Allow

1 point for each (a) response.

3 points for each (b) response.

5 points for each (c) response.

The total should be between 20 and 100 points.

The score can reveal much about HRD in an organization and in particular the attitude toward evaluation and measurement. A perfect score of 100 is probably unachievable. It represents utopia and is an ultimate goal of many HRD departments. Conversely, a score of 20 reveals an ineffective organization with inappropriate methods. The test has been administered to several hundred HRD staff members and managers. The scores can be analyzed by examining these four ranges:

Score Range	Analysis of Score
81–100	This organization represents results-based education and training in action. There is little room for improvement and little need to take any additional concentrated efforts to improve evaluation of the HRD function. Management support is great. Departments with this rating are leaders in this important field of evaluation and setting examples for others. This organization should be extremely effective with this attitude toward HRD and evaluation.
61–80	This organization is probably better than average in HRD evaluation. There is room for improvement, but present efforts appear to be headed in the right direction. There is some attention to obtaining results and evaluation of programs. Some methods appear to be appropriate, but additional emphasis is needed to position HRD to contribute more in the future. Management support is moderate.
41–60	Improvement is needed in this organization. The attitude and approach to HRD evaluation are less than desirable. Present methods are ineffective. Emphasis needs to be placed on securing the appropriate management support to change the philosophy of the organization.
20–40	In this organization there is little or no concern for measuring results of the HRD function. The HRD function is ineffective and needs improvement if it is to survive. Urgent attention is needed from top management to change the approach of the HRD function.

HOW "GOOD" IS GOOD CUSTOMER SERVICE?

Harriet Diamond

Harriet Diamond *is president of Diamond Associates, Multi-Faceted Training and Development (123 Quimby Street, Westfield, New Jersey, 07090, 908-232-2075), a firm that designs and delivers customized training programs and consulting services spanning all areas of communication and management skills. Harriet is the author of six published writing skills books (Barron's Educational Series, Inc.) and numerous published articles on oral and written communication. Diamond Associates works with industries including banking, pharmaceutical, transportation, utility, retail, health care, and casino and hotel.*

OVERVIEW

The Good Customer Service Inventory is designed to help everyone in an organization assess her or his communication skills and styles when interacting with customers. Respondents obtain feedback from four questions:

1. What is your level of patience and acceptance?
2. Are you a team player?
3. How do you feel about your job? How are you perceived?
4. How do your interpersonal skills rate?

THE GOOD CUSTOMER SERVICE INVENTORY

This questionnaire is designed to give you a picture of your communication style and skills as you interact with customers. It is for your eyes only; be honest. Answer truthfully, not the way that you think you should answer.

Circle the number of the description that best corresponds.

5, strongly agree;   4, agree;   3, indifferent;
2, disagree;   1, strongly disagree

1. If I answer a customer's question quickly and accurately, I have done my job as well as anyone should expect.   5 4 3 2 1

2. When a customer is rude or impatient with me, I have every right to be rude right back.   5 4 3 2 1

3. When a customer is rude or impatient with me, I cannot be rude, but I certainly don't have to go out of my way.   5 4 3 2 1

4. My co-workers who say that if I smile at everyone I will look like a "grinning idiot" are *wrong*.   5 4 3 2 1

5. I resent it when a customer asks for the "nice person" who helped the last time.   5 4 3 2 1

6. If I am on the phone and a customer approaches, I cannot just hang up; the customer has to wait.   5 4 3 2 1

7. I appreciate being thanked by customers.   5 4 3 2 1

8. I appreciate being complimented by my manager.   5 4 3 2 1

9. I am not in a position to compliment my co-workers on how they do their jobs.   5 4 3 2 1

10. When I see the manager compliment my co-workers, I wonder whether I will get recognition for something I did.   5 4 3 2 1

11. My personal appearance does not affect how customers react to me.   5 4 3 2 1

12. I don't come to work to get grief. If people dump on me, they cannot expect me to take it.   5 4 3 2 1

13. Some people just like to hear themselves talk. At some point, I can just tune them out.   5 4 3 2 1

14. Some types of people really irritate me.   5 4 3 2 1

15. People who are always friendly *don't* seem phony.   5 4 3 2 1

16. People cannot tell when I am having a bad day.   5   4   3   2   1

17. If I have a problem with one customer, I have a short fuse with the next.   5   4   3   2   1

18. I enjoy talking to a lot of people throughout the day.   5   4   3   2   1

19. If I am in the middle of something that I have to finish, I don't have to tell customers I will be right with them. They know I see them.   5   4   3   2   1

20. I give faster service to someone in a business suit than I do to someone who looks unemployed or retired; they are probably not in a hurry.   5   4   3   2   1

21. I feel good about myself when I solve a customer's problem.   5   4   3   2   1

22. If I see a customer looking lost, I don't ask if I can help because, if customers *need* help, they usually ask.   5   4   3   2   1

23. I don't give my name on the phone, but if people ask, I will tell them.   5   4   3   2   1

24. I would rather try to figure things out on my own than ask advice of a co-worker.   5   4   3   2   1

THE GOOD CUSTOMER SERVICE INVENTORY
SCORE SHEET

Scoring: Write your score in the space to the right of each number. Add the total of the numbers in each group for the corresponding question. Read how to interpret your results.

What's your level of patience and acceptance?

2	_____
3	_____
12	_____
13	_____
14	_____
17	_____
Total	_____

6–12   You understand the secrets of the service industry. The better you treat angry customers, the nicer they become.

13–30   You tend to take customers' impatience personally. Often they are defensive for fear of being brushed off. Your best defense is to be friendly, listen, and offer assistance.

Are you a team player?

5	_____
9	_____
10	_____
11	_____
24	_____
Total	_____

5–10   Your open, sharing nature is ideal for your company's positive customer relations environment.

11–25   This is not a competitive environment and you may have a competitive streak. Look over these questions again. Think about what holds you back from sharing ideas, giving support, or asking for help. Use the support systems within your work environment.

How do you feel about your job? How are you perceived?

4	_____
7	_____
8	_____
15	_____
16	_____
18	_____
21	_____
Total	_____

15–35 Your positive attitude shows through.

7–14 You may need to work harder to become comfortable in the service industry. Before you can change your actions, you will have to reassess your views.

How do your interpersonal skills rate?

1	_____
6	_____
19	_____
20	_____
22	_____
23	_____
Total	_____

6–12 Your genuine concern allows you to *put yourself in your customer's shoes.*

13–30 Review your answers to these questions. Can you imagine yourself as the customer? How would you want someone to act toward you?

116

IS YOUR SELF-DIRECTED TEAM WORKING?

Robert Lesniak and Olga Blouch

Robert J. Lesniak, *Ph.D., is coordinator of the master's degree in education, training, and development major at the Pennsylvania State University at Harrisburg (77 West Harrisburg Pike, Middletown, PA 17057-4898, RJL1@PSUVM.PSU.edu). He has been a contributor to publications including* **Models for HRD Practice: The Academic Guide.** *He is an active member of the Academy for HRD and the Central Pennsylvania Chapter of the American Society for Training and Development.* **Olga Blouch** *is a master's student at the Pennsylvania State University at Harrisburg.*

OVERVIEW

Many companies are implementing self-directed teams into their work process as a strategy to meet the identified goals of the organization. The success or failure of a work team's ability to attain the company goals depends on the team's ability to interact in a supportive environment with positive, forward-thinking leadership.

The Self-directed Team Survey asks team members for their perceptions of the way that their work group interacts, functions within its organizational environment, and follows its leadership. After individual team members have taken *The Self-directed Team Survey,* they are given questions to discuss to consider factors affecting their performance. A list of processing questions that covers both the organizational and training barriers to the effectiveness of self-directed teams helps members to evaluate what factors might be inhibiting the group from performing at their maximum potential.

THE SELF-DIRECTED TEAM SURVEY

How often do the following statements apply to your team? Circle the number that best corresponds to your response.

Team Interaction	Never 0%	Seldom 25%	Sometimes 50%	Often 75%
1. Everyone is working toward a common goal.	0	1	2	3
2. People feel free to express thoughts, feelings, and ideas.	0	1	2	3
3. Members trust one another.	0	1	2	3
4. Members listen to each other.	0	1	2	3
5. Members cooperate with each other.	0	1	2	3
6. Teams of people do tasks that require coordination and interdependence.	0	1	2	3
7. Each member participates in decisions.	0	1	2	3
8. Members feel comfortable coaching each other.	0	1	2	3
9. Conflict is accepted and handled.	0	1	2	3
10. The team evaluates how well it is doing.	0	1	2	3
Your score for each column:	____	____	____	____

Your team interaction composite score (sum of column scores): ____

Team Environment	Never 0%	Seldom 25%	Sometimes 50%	Often 75%
1. Positive attitudes exist.	0	1	2	3
2. The work atmosphere is comfortable and tension-free.	0	1	2	3
3. Members try new ideas.	0	1	2	3
4. Deadlines are clearly defined.	0	1	2	3
5. Members know their individual responsibilities within the team.	0	1	2	3
6. Meetings are efficient and results-oriented.	0	1	2	3
7. Team members rotate team tasks.	0	1	2	3
8. The team attends training as a group.	0	1	2	3
9. Team training is ongoing.	0	1	2	3
10. The team understands its relationship to the whole organization.	0	1	2	3

Your score for each column: _____ _____ _____ _____

Your team environment composite score (sum of column scores): _____

Team Leadership	Never 0%	Seldom 25%	Sometimes 50%	Often 75%
1. Everyone is kept informed.	0	1	2	3
2. The leader does not dominate the group.	0	1	2	3
3. The leader provides feedback to members.	0	1	2	3
4. The team manages its own budget.	0	1	2	3
5. The team controls its own work schedule.	0	1	2	3
6. Management supports team decisions.	0	1	2	3
7. Management makes sure that the team has adequate resources.	0	1	2	3
8. Executives, managers, and supervisors receive training on the team concept.	0	1	2	3
9. The team deals directly with people at all levels of the company.	0	1	2	3
10. The team is permitted to make changes in work processes without going through multiple levels of management.	0	1	2	3

Your score for each column: ____ ____ ____ ____

Your team leadership composite score (sum of column scores): ____

The Self-directed Team Survey does not have norms. You are expected to set your own standards for how well your team is working. If you and your fellow team members agree that you are not working as well as you would like, discuss the following questions.

Processing Questions for Self-directed Teams

Is your team working as well as it could? Review this list of common organizational barriers to self-directed teams and see how many apply to your work group.

1. Team members lack sufficient training.
2. Supervisors resist change.
3. Technological systems are incompatible.
4. Implementation is too fast.
5. Management is unsupportive.
6. Unions are unsupportive.

Is your team fully prepared to be self-directed? Ask yourself if your team members have received training in the following areas:

1. Team design concepts
2. Listening and giving feedback
3. Techniques for handling conflict and reaching consensus
4. Diversity
5. Presentation skills
6. Meeting facilitation

In what ways can you help your self-directed team to be more productive?

HELPFUL HANDOUTS

In this section of *The 1996 McGraw-Hill Team and Organization Development Sourcebook*, you will find seven "helpful" handouts. These handouts cover topics such as:

✓ Team meetings.

✓ Customer service.

✓ Organizational change.

✓ Team development.

✓ Roles of team members.

These handouts can be used in a variety of ways:

✓ As participant materials in training programs

✓ As discussion documents during team meetings

✓ As coaching tools or job aids

✓ As information to be read by you or shared with a colleague

All of the handouts are designed as succinct descriptions of important issues or skills when developing teams or organizations. They are formatted for quick, easily understood reading. (You may want to keep these handouts handy as reminders or checklists by posting them in your work area.) Most important of all, they contain nuggets of practical advice!

Preceding each handout is a brief overview of its contents and uses. The handouts themselves are on a separate pages to make reproduction convenient.

It is helpful to read these handouts *actively*. Highlight points that are important to you or push you to do further thinking. Identify content that needs further clarification. Challenge yourself to come up with examples that illustrate the key points. Urge others to be active consumers of these handouts as well.

PROCESS DECISIONS EVERY TEAM MUST MAKE

Cynthia Solomon

Cynthia Solomon, *Ph.D., is a technical program specialist for FERMCO, an environmental restoration company in Ohio (6469 Fountains Blvd., West Chester, OH 45069, 513-777-5435). Cindy had led or designed organizational and professional development projects for her employer, the health care industry, and professional organizations, and chairs the professional development committee of a chapter of the National Management Association. She authored* **TQM in Dietetics and Nutrition Services** *(Wolf Rinke Associates, 1993).*

OVERVIEW

A team is more than a group. To be effective, a team must come to some decision about the process by which it will function so that it is, as a whole, greater than the sum of the parts. Process decisions are those made by the team about how they will work together. Process decisions are separate from the substantive (or content) decisions of their specific project.

This helpful handout is a simple checklist for a team leader to ensure that supportive process decisions are made, understood, and agreed to by the team. Teams work best if they share a common understanding of these processes before they begin to work, rather than waiting until a difference or obstacle that requires resolution occurs. Use this handout as a reference tool the next time that you or a co-worker leads a team.

PROCESS DECISIONS EVERY TEAM MUST MAKE

Scope of the Assignment and the Deliverables

Ensure that everyone understands the assignment and what product or services the team is expected to deliver to the customer. This understanding helps the team focus on results that will be valued. Deliverables could be a plan, a recommendation, a solution to a problem, a document, and so on. The team could take some time to discuss the characteristics of the deliverable and be certain that the customer agrees to it.

Roles and Responsibilities

This is a *big* one! Don't make assumptions that everyone understands what is expected of them. And don't make assumptions that all the work of the team will be completed by someone unless you decide in advance who will do what. Teams have leadership positions, task positions, and support positions. Decide what the team needs and who will perform each task.

Formal Meeting Frequency, Date, Times, Location

Can you establish a standing time, dates, and location for meetings throughout the life of the team project? This advance information helps team members to plan their availability for team meetings and makes the scheduling of meetings easier for the team member who will do the scheduling. If you cannot establish a standing meeting, conclude each meeting with an agreement on the date, time, and location of the next meeting.

Informal or Subgroup Meetings

Informal or subgroup meetings consist of members of the larger team who meet to discuss the project, or one aspect of it, aside from the entire team. The team needs to recognize that such groups may or may not be needed and if planning and decisions may be completed by such groups aside from the whole group. This avoids an instance in which several team members informally decide to meet, discuss the team activity, and develop a proposal on their own without the acknowledgment of the entire team that their work would be supportive, rather than viewed (and often resisted) as a separatist activity.

Need for Team Records: Agenda, Minutes, Action Items

What kind of agenda does the team want? How far in advance of each meeting should team members have a copy of the agenda? Who will be responsible for planning the agenda? How can team members place items on the agenda? What kind of meeting minutes does the team require? Should the minutes contain action items for individuals or records of decisions, motions, and results? To whom should meeting minutes be sent? Who shall be responsible for taking and distributing meeting minutes? In what format shall minutes be written?

Plan of Action

Teams are generally given an assignment with some defined deliverable. The team develops the plan of action that it will take. A skillful facilitator leads the team into an identification of all the elements of a good plan, how the elements will fit together, who will be responsible for each element, and, if desired, the schedule by which each element will be completed.

Manner in Which Different Opinions and Preferences Are Presented to and Received by the Team

Depending on the composition of the group, individuals who are new to a team should come to an understanding of the acceptance of different opinions and preferences and how to offer them. This often is a reflection of the organizational culture in which the team exists. The team facilitator should lead the group in a discussion of the value of differences and lead the team in agreeing on how differences will be resolved. This discussion, up front, encourages freedom to think and to contribute diverse ideas and ultimately results in a more comprehensive approach to the team's work. Some team members who do not have this issue resolved may settle back into an accepting role on the team and defer to the dominant personalities. Their value-added may never reach the table.

Manner in Which Decisions Are Made

Does the team want to formally vote on decisions, come to agreement through discussion, or engage in any other decision model?

Manner in Which Team Members Will Be Updated on Team Progress

The team is stronger if all members share the same information in a timely fashion. A team can become fragmented and ineffective if some members of the team are in the know while others are not. Meeting minutes and agenda are the most common form of updates; however, the team may decide that intermediate phone calls, memos, e-mail messages, or other means may be helpful and supportive to the team members.

WHY PEOPLE RESIST ORGANIZATIONAL CHANGE

Ed Betof

Ed Betof, *Ed.D., is senior vice-president of MC Associates (Mellon Bank Center, 1735 Market Street, 43rd Floor, Philadelphia, PA 19103, 215-563-7800), a consulting firm specializing in organizational change and leadership development. Ed is an adjunct faculty member of the Center for Creative Leadership and the Human Resource Planning Society. He is the lead author of* Just Promoted! Surviving and Thriving in Your First Twelve Months as a Manager *(McGraw-Hill).*

OVERVIEW

Why are some organizational change efforts successful and others crashing failures? What are the underlying forces that serve to work against your best-laid plans?

The following handout lists the reasons why people resist organizational change, no matter how well intentioned, practical, beneficial, or reasonable these changes may be. Keep this handout nearby the next time that you are asked to be an agent for organizational change, and you will be better prepared for the resistance that is likely to come your way.

WHY PEOPLE RESIST ORGANIZATIONAL CHANGE*

Many people in leadership positions have to overcome resistance to the organizational change that they are trying to implement. Before the resistance can be overcome, it needs to be understood. Listed next are 12 of the most common reasons why people resist organizational change.

1. *Organizational homeostasis.* Like living organisms, individuals, groups, and organizations tend to level off at a steady state or revert to earlier norms. This tendency to fall back is called *organizational homeostasis* and is common in all change efforts. Homeostasis manifests itself in several guises. One is the tendency for organizations that have improved their standard of quality to fall back from that standard. Homeostasis can also affect how the work is done. Many companies, having spent considerably on a new computer system, software, and training, are stunned to find employees more comfortable with their old ways.

2. *Illusion of impotence.* People tend to attribute much greater power to others than they do to themselves. They often see themselves as isolated and unable to affect change. Individuals often see others as much more able to take action and to overcome barriers. Ironically, people will frequently identify each other as having much more power or influence than they see themselves as having. The key is for many in the organization to feel the ability to influence positive change and work with others to do so.

3. *Selective perception.* Simply stated, perceiving is believing. Perception gives personal meaning to what we experience. People filter the events around them through the selective screens of their needs and values. They will see and hear what they are predisposed to perceive and believe their perceptions. It has been said that whenever two people interact there are seemingly six people present:

   ✓ Each person as he sees himself

   ✓ Each person as she or he views the other and the events around them

   ✓ Each person as he or she really is

   As a force acting against change or growth, selective perception can be critical, since people see what they want to see and what agrees with their perceptions.

*Adapted from Edward Betof and Frederic Harwood, *Just Promoted! Surviving and Thriving in Your First Twelve Months as a Manager,* New York: McGraw-Hill, 1992.

4. *Rule of modeling.* Beginning at infancy, we learn how things are done through modeling, habit, and reinforcement. A type of programming occurs. The rule of modeling says that we tend to do first that which has been modeled for us. We will usually act as we have seen others around us behave in the past.

5. *Vested interests.* It is often a shock to new managers to learn that people do not do something even though it is right and just. People do not always do the right thing, but rather they often act out of self-interest and what is best for them.

6. *Lack of monitoring, control, or evaluation tools to maximize follow-up.* Leaders must follow up on decisions, be accountable, and hold others to their responsibilities and agreements. Leaders will fail if they do not monitor implementation of plans, exert control when implementation gets off track, or evaluate the effectiveness of the plans.

7. *Lack of involvement and ownership in problem solving the organization's critical positions.* Many new leaders are reluctant to involve their people or give them authority and power. The people who hold the organization's critical positions in management and the work force must feel a sense of ownership for the organization's new ideas. They must participate in developing and implementing these ideas, and their input must receive consideration. Everyone must feel heard if they try to contribute.

8. *Failure to identify the issues to be addressed and specific action steps to be taken.* A very difficult part of addressing change is to move from the identification of a problem (what is wrong) to the identification of a solution and the implementation of action steps. These steps include timetables and milestones for improvement. Here, being specific with the who, what, where, and when will be very helpful.

9. *Escape from accountability.* As opposed to high-performing organizations, many people in low- or moderately performing organizations choose not to be held accountable for their work or for efforts to improve the organization. A cheerful balance must be achieved with employees when creating the conditions for high motivation. Monitoring, measuring, and accountability work well with reinforcement, recognition, and reward.

10. *Lack of positive peer support and peer pressure.* Organizational change requires developing a culture that supports change from within. This means that the workforce must be convinced that its best interests coincide with what is best for the organization. Some of the most convincing arguments come from colleagues and peers who understand the positive implications in strengthening an organization.

A common mistake is not getting the workforce involved in the organizational improvement process early enough. To get them involved after they have substantive grievances tends to encourage them to coalesce into a kind of mutual support group pitted against management. Better to get them involved early in the process, serving on committees with management, and not on worker committees that make recommendations to management. Build consensus, not conflict, and bridges, not walls.

11. *Inadequate pressure to improve.* Generally, the tension or pressure to change and grow is not strong in organizations. People will not change if there is little impetus to do so. Organizations can benefit from pressure from within or outside the organization. This structural tension or cognitive dissonance is the tension that people feel when they realize the difference between what actually exists and what could be. The pressure can come from a variety of sources. External pressure comes from competition, from clients and customers, from leaders and stockholders. Internal pressure can come from leadership, from productivity or profitability data, from peer pressure, or from competition for internal resources. Individuals often feel their own internalized pressure when they realize the difference between what actually exists and what should be.

12. *Too much, too soon.* Organizations are capable of managing only so much change at one time. Change disrupts the work flow, slowing or bringing things to a halt. Well-managed change affects the organization while not seriously disrupting the ongoing work. The key is to work on one or two priorities at a time to build momentum and a pattern of successful implementation. The conclusions from your diagnostic work will provide a firm basis for your priorities.

SIX STEPS TO SUPERIOR SERVICE

Robert Scully and Karen Cherwony

Robert Scully, *D.B.A., is academic coordinator of business programs at Barry University. He has 13 years of college teaching experience in business administration and 10 years of business experience in management, finance, marketing, and corporate training. He can be reached at 1095 NW 117th Avenue, Coral Springs, FL 33071, 305-346-0583.* **Karen Cherwony,** *Ed.D, as director of human resource development at Temple University (Personnel Services, 204A U.S.B., 1601 North Broad Street, Philadelphia, PA 19122, 215-204-1669), is responsible for a variety of training and organizational development programs at the university and its hospital, including the A+ Service Program, one of the first customer service initiatives in higher education.*

OVERVIEW

The fact that superior service provides an organization with a competitive edge is an undisputed reality that most managers readily endorse. However, creating and maintaining a high level of service remains an unattainable goal for many organizations. *Six Steps to Superior Service* provides a blueprint for building or improving an organization's customer service. It was inspired by *The Service Triangle* (Albrecht and Zemke, 1985), which suggested that outstanding service requires more than competent and caring front-line employees. The service circle given at the end of the handout identifies the interconnected elements that service leaders need to proactively manage to successfully attract and retain satisfied customers.

SIX STEPS TO SUPERIOR SERVICE

The six steps to superior service described here are presented as sequential managerial tasks, but the circle diagram suggests that managing for service excellence is a never-ending, integrated, comprehensive, and cyclical process revolving around the customer. The customer is both central and connected to each of the six steps. To maintain the customer as the central source of attraction, it is essential to have a clear and thorough understanding of both your current and potential customers.

Answer these questions before learning more about the service cycle: What is the demographic makeup of your current customers? Have they changed over time? How will they be changing in the future? What are their service needs now and in the future? Are you prepared to deal with more diverse customers? Is there an understanding of the difference between external and internal customers and a recognition that those who serve external customers need service from co-workers? How do you assess customer needs, expectations, preferences, and satisfaction? How do you educate customers to be smart consumers? How do you attract new customers?

Once you have a clear idea as to who your customers are and have a sense of both their current and future needs, you can analyze how to provide them with superior service. The six steps necessary to support your customer are as follows:

1. *Standards.* Based on the needs of your customers, prepare a mission statement to define your commitment to quality service. Set clear, concise, observable, and realistic standards for service that establish service goals, communicate expectations, and integrate management tools such as job descriptions, interview questions, training efforts, and performance appraisals. Procedural expectations, which deal with service delivery systems and how things get done (for example, all calls to customers will be returned within 24 hours; no one will wait longer than 15 minutes), and personal standards, which are the interpersonal attitudes, behaviors, and verbal skills (for example, state the company name and your name when answering the telephone; sneakers and jeans are not permitted dress), should be detailed and clearly communicated to everyone (Martin, 1989). Standards should address the five factors that customers use to evaluate service: reliability, responsiveness, assurance, empathy, and tangibles (Anderson and Zemke, 1991).

2. *Strategy.* Fulfilling your service mission and implementing quality service standards require a strategic plan and leadership to carry them out. Often this is nothing short of a commitment to total culture change in the organization. Strategic moves include the following:

   ✓ Conducting a service audit to identify the gap between standards that you aspire to meet and current levels of service

   ✓ Involving customers and service providers in defining customer needs and setting and implementing standards

   ✓ Changing, adding, and deleting products and services to be more in align with customer needs

   ✓ Revising job descriptions, hiring procedures, training programs, performance appraisals, and reward and compensation systems to reflect a new service emphasis

   ✓ Rethinking traditional organizational structures such as departmental boundaries and reporting lines to allow more employee involvement and greater cross-departmental cooperation.

3. *Systems.* Evaluate how user-friendly your service systems are. Have policies and procedures been designed for the convenience of the customer, not the organization and its staff? Telephone systems, return policies, problem and complaint resolution procedures, hours of operation, and billing and collection procedures are but a few of the many systems that can malfunction and result in customer dissatisfaction.

4. *Supervision.* Quality service requires quality supervision of the service providers. Effective supervisors set high performance expectations and hold people accountable for their actions. They are on top of situations and anticipate problems. They respect, empower, and support their staff. Quality supervision begins with developing job descriptions, which include service standards, and hiring front-line workers that have both the technical and interpersonal skills necessary to do the job right. The supervisor has to be a coach, counselor, and trainer who identifies performance problems and provides the feedback and resources that workers need to improve their ability. The supervisor also actively solicits employees' input and feedback. The most successful supervisors are cheerleaders who motivate, recognize and reward excellence. They transmit vigor, vitality, and a sense of accomplishment and purpose. And, probably most importantly, they model quality service in their interactions with customers and employees. They "walk their talk."

5. *Staff.* No matter how well thought out the standards are, how comprehensive the strategy, or how well greased the system, it is still the front-line workers who can make or break customers' service experiences and impressions. Service stars must be hired or home grown. To hire service stars,

✓ Delineate the ideal characteristics and skills required.

✓ Expand your recruitment efforts to locate the best candidates.

✓ Conduct a thorough interview and evaluate the candidates on public relations and interpersonal skills, not just technical competencies.

Developing service stars requires the quality supervision discussed as well as an organizational commitment to value, reward, and empower employees. Dissatisfied workers may communicate their dissatisfaction to customers. Even if they don't, employees are quick to recognize the hypocrisy of an organization that professes to be service-oriented and concerned about customers, but treats its own employees poorly. Respect and empower employees by providing timely access to accurate information, encouraging and structuring opportunities for employees to suggest service improvements, and granting the authority to make decisions on behalf of customers even if there is some risk of their making mistakes.

6. *Support.* Keeping superior service alive and well is an ongoing challenge that requires continual attention. Front-line staff, supervisors, and managers all need to be supported and reminded of the organization's commitment to quality and customers. This can occur through educational efforts such as newsletters, speakers, and training programs.

Service audits, which include customer and employee surveys, suggestion boxes, and focus groups, naturally lead to a revision of standards and strategies and the identification of system problems. These in turn foster other change efforts, such as quality improvement circles, cross-functional process improvement teams, reengineering, and diversity programs.

Service excellence is not a destination but a never-ending journey with many curves, potholes, and other barriers that can impede your progress. However, if you are prepared with a map and the other supports that you need, it is a trip worth taking.

REFERENCES

Albrecht, K., and R. Zemke. 1985. *Service America!* Homewood, IL: Dow Jones-Irwin.

Anderson, K., and R. Zemke. 1991. *Delivering Knock Your Socks off Service.* New York: AMACOM.

Martin, W. B. 1989. *Managing Quality Customer Service.* Los Altos, CA: Crisp Publications.

Zemke, R. 1988. Supervising service workers. *Training,* 25(10), 62–66.

Zemke, R., and C. Bell. 1990. Service recovery: Doing it right the second time. *Training,* 27(6), 42–48.

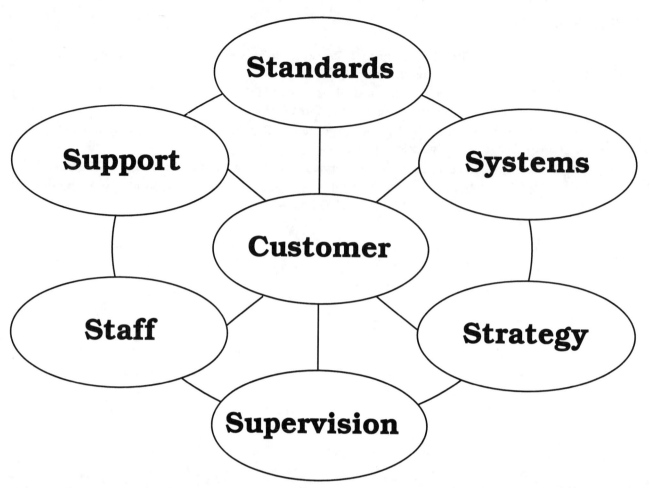

Figure 26.1. Service Circle: Six Steps to Superior Service.

USING A PARTICIPATION AGENDA FOR TEAM MEETINGS

Cynthia Solomon

Cynthia Solomon, *Ph.D., is a technical program specialist for FERMCO, an environmental restoration company in Ohio (6469 Fountains Blvd., West Chester, OH 45069, 513-777-5435). Cindy had led or designed organizational and professional development projects for her employer, the health care industry, and professional organizations and chairs the professional development committee of a chapter of the National Management Association. She authored* **TQM in Dietetics and Nutrition Services** *(Wolf Rinke Associates, 1993).*

OVERVIEW

Effective, productive team meetings are most often the result of the quality of individual participation at the meeting. A meeting that is a report to a group for information and discussion purposes depends on the preparation and delivery of information by one person *to* the group. However, if the meeting is a working or planning session in which individuals are expected to contribute to the team's effort, advance notice of the meeting agenda helps members to prepare. A *participation agenda* like the one that follows is helpful to enhance meeting participation among team members.

The objectives of this handout are to

✓ Distinguish between a participation agenda and an informational agenda.

✓ List benefits of a participation agenda.

✓ Illustrate how to write a participation agenda.

USING A PARTICIPATION AGENDA FOR TEAM MEETINGS

A *participation agenda* is a meeting agenda in which team members are expected to participate in reporting, discussion, planning, problem solving, and decision making. Advance notice of the particular issues allows the team to prepare. The agenda is specific as to the issues, questions, and decisions that will be addressed during the meeting. The advantages of this type of meeting agenda are as follows:

✓ It makes meeting members aware of the issues, questions, and decisions that will be addressed in advance of the meeting so that they can collect their own information and thoughts, formulate questions that they want to raise, and attend the meeting in a more informed manner.

✓ It keeps the meeting on task; that is, it keeps the meeting focused on those issues, questions, and decisions that the team must consider.

By comparison, an *information agenda* is a meeting agenda that lists those items that will be reported to provide information to the group. Generally, one or several people prepare a presentation of the information, but the majority of attendants are there to listen.

An *information agenda* has most or all of the following usual characteristics:

✓ Date, time, and location of the meeting
✓ Title of the group that is meeting
✓ Brief list of topics that will be covered

The following is an example of an *information agenda.* For illustration purposes, the agenda is written for an advisory committee for a local technical college.

XYZ PROGRAM ADVISORY COMMITTEE
2:00–4:00 PM
Central Meeting Room

1.	Welcome and Introductions	G. Smith, Program Director
2.	Enrollment	
3.	Curriculum	
4.	Report on Graduates	
5.	Report on New Laboratory Acquisitions for the Program	

This informational agenda accomplishes the following:

✓ The meeting is correctly identified in terms of title, date, place, and time.

✓ The attendants at the meeting will come to listen to reports on each of the agenda items by a member of the faculty.

✓ There is no indication as to exactly what the participants at the meeting should do. How should they prepare for the meeting? What input will they have at the meeting? Are they there just to receive information? This agenda would appear to require nothing from the participants except to sit and listen.

The same agenda has been rewritten as a *participation agenda.* As you read and compare this sample with the information agenda, see if you can identify any difference in your reaction if you were an invited participant to the meeting. Notes are commentary on the agenda item and are not a part of the actual agenda; they are entered here for instructional purposes.

XYZ PROGRAM ADVISORY COMMITTEE
2:00–4:00 PM
Central Meeting Room

1. Welcome and Introductions   G. Smith, Program Director

   We have several new members to this committee. At your suggestion, we have invited representatives from the health department and the library.

   Note: This agenda item lets members know that a previous suggestion was acted on. It is also good manners to introduce new members to a group.

2. Enrollment

   Our enrollment is still at 25 students. All the students are full-time day students. We still feel that there are employed persons who would like to enroll. We would like a discussion of alternative scheduling options.

   Note: Members may have some ideas that would help the college schedule or market its programs to persons who are employed during the day.

3. Curriculum

   The college has received a grant to bring in an FTE curriculum specialist to develop new course materials next year. What skills should we focus on to make our graduates more valuable?

   Note: The members of this committee include some employers of graduates. Who best to ask what skills they would like to see in graduates that they might employ?

4. Report on Graduates

   Of the 15 graduates from last year, 12 were employed in hospitals. Our program is designed to prepare graduates for employment in public health, long-term care, and clinics. Are there promotional activities we should be using to broaden the areas where graduates are employed?

   Note: If the committee is well representative of the community, there could be some community outreach links made here between the college and potential sites of employment for graduates.

5. Report on New Laboratory Acquisitions for the Program

Our laboratory is now equipped with five new computers. We will be giving a 15-minute demonstration of our software at this meeting. Our interest is in getting your ideas on work simulations that we could use with this new equipment. Your ideas, please.

Notes: Another example of participants who know what skills are needed could recommend real work experiences and scenarios for students to practice. Maybe one of the committee members would volunteer to work with the faculty to develop scenarios or practice sessions on the computer.

Next, we give six tips for preparing a participation agenda:

1. Identify the date, time, and location of the meeting.

2. List the names of those who have been invited. Sometimes knowing the names of the persons who will attend may encourage others to attend.

3. List the general topics to be covered using a brief descriptive title. In the preceding sample the general topics are

Welcome and Introductions

Enrollment

Curriculum

Report on Graduates

Report on New Laboratory Acquisitions for the Program

4. Allocate the time allowed for each topic. This helps the meeting facilitator to guide the group so that the majority of time is not spent in a too detailed discussion of the first one or two topics, with little time left for the remainder of the meeting.

5. For each general topic, think of the specific areas that should be discussed. Is there some background information that must be reported first? Are there any critical questions for which the organization having the meeting would like potential answers? Are there any creative ideas you would like to have from the participants? Would you like the participants to perform some service for the organization, such as make contacts with another organization, make some resources available, or provide expertise?

6. Keep the agenda as brief as possible—one page is best. While the participation agenda encourages giving as much advance information as possible about the subjects and issues to be discussed, it should not be burdensome.

TIPS FOR TEAM BRAINSTORMING

Cynthia Denton-Ade

As head of CDA Performance Systems (9850 Natick Road, Burke, VA 22015, 703-503-6679, CompuServe 74534,1077), **Cynthia Denton-Ade** *has 18 years experience designing and developing technical and management training. She works with industry and government clients to design training that maximizes student participation and learning. Cynthia conducts many workshops each year in instructor training, communications, and problem solving. She has held several offices in the National Society for Performance and Instruction and has won awards for her service.*

OVERVIEW

Brainstorming is an effective way to produce a large number of ideas in a short period of time. The technique was developed by Alex Osborn in 1941 as a way to separate the generation of ideas from the evaluation of those ideas. Successful team brainstorming creates an uninhibited atmosphere in which participants can list, combine, improve, and stretch ideas.

This helpful handout lists important guidelines to follow when conducting team brainstorming sessions. It also suggests a step-by-step process to use in generating and evaluating ideas for maximum results.

TIPS FOR TEAM BRAINSTORMING

The word *brainstorming* is often misinterpreted to mean any activity by which a team generates ideas. Actually, it is a clearly designed procedure with a specific set of guidelines. These guidelines are designed to encourage the flow of ideas and overcome blocks to creative thinking. When a team follows them, the creative potential of the group is released.

Team Brainstorming Guidelines

✓ *Go for quantity.* Research has shown that quantity breeds quality. In other words, the more ideas that you come up with, the more likely that you get a truly good idea. The goal of brainstorming is to generate as many ideas as possible. Record all ideas as they pop up, no matter how similar they may seem.

Use these two go-for-quantity options:

1. *Set a time limit.* For example, ask the group to think of as many ideas as possible in 15 minutes. Then give them another 5 minutes and then another until they run out of ideas. Research shows that people often generate their best ideas during the later portions of brainstorming, so don't be afraid to push the group for "one more idea."

2. *Set a quota of ideas.* For example, ask them to generate 30 ideas. When the group has met the quota, then ask for 10 more. Continue this process until you are sure that the group has run out of ideas.

✓ *Suspend judgment.* We tend to judge new ideas instantly and are often incorrect. If you criticize, judge, or comment on ideas as they are generated, the flow of ideas will slow down or stop completely. Ban comments that inhibit brainstorming such as "That idea just won't work," or "We can't afford that," or "We've tried that one before."

✓ *Be freewheeling.* Encourage any ideas, the wilder the better. As psychologist Sidney Parnes said, "It is easier to tame a wild idea than to invigorate a dull one." If the group is being too cautious, you can ask, "What are the wildest, most outrageous ideas we can come up with?"

✓ *Piggyback.* Creativity always involves the manipulation of ideas. Encourage participants to add, modify, or elaborate on each other's ideas. Use questions that allow people to see links between different ideas, even if they seem to be unrelated.

Utilize these two piggyback options:

1. Use idea extending questions such as, "What else can this be used for?", "Are there new ways to use this idea?", "How could it be changed or adapted?", and "How might we make this idea larger or smaller?"

2. Encourage participants to force connections between unrelated ideas. This helps people to look for relationships and provides a different perspective on the problem.

The Two Phases of Brainstorming

Once the general guidelines are known and in place, it pays to follow a structured sequence of steps so that team brainstorming is really effective. These steps involve two phases: *idea generation* and *idea evaluation*. To maximize idea generation:

✓ *Select the problem.* State the problem in a way that allows the most possibilities for generating ideas. Try beginning the question with, "In what ways might we …" For example, "In what ways might we get along better at work (handle customer complaints, or meet deadlines)?"

✓ *Choose the participants.* The ideal number of people to include in a brainstorming session is between five and twelve. Ideally the group will have a positive outlook about the problem and feel comfortable about sharing its ideas with others. It is best to include people who are of relatively equal status. Nothing kills a brainstorming session more than the strong opinion of authority. Omit observers; everyone who attends should be an active participant.

✓ *Prepare the environment.* Ideas can be generated only if the atmosphere is comfortable and informal. Research has shown that movement stimulates creative thinking, so allow space for the participants to move around. Decide if you will record the ideas on flip chart paper or on overhead transparencies. Use flip chart paper if you want to post the ideas on the wall so that everyone can see. Use transparencies if you want to photocopy the pages and distribute them to the participants.

✓ *Post the rules of brainstorming.* Introduce or review the brainstorming rules and post them on the wall so that they can be seen by all the participants.

✓ *Select a recorder.* Assign someone to record all ideas generated by the group. Have the recorder write down every idea, even if it is a restatement of previous ideas. If a thought is not recorded, it will very likely disappear. Encourage the recorder to use symbols and stick figures, as well as written phrases. The concept is to find colorful, interesting, and graphic ways to illustrate an idea. When the flip chart page is full, post it on the wall.

✓ *Conduct a brainstorming warm-up activity.* Before you conduct a session on the real problem, begin with a warm-up session. This will start the creative juices flowing and help participants to practice brainstorming. Select a fun subject like "In what ways might we use a third arm, if we had one?" or "What are all the possible uses of a Styrofoam cup?"

✓ *Post the brainstorming problem and start the session.* Allow 20 to 30 minutes for the group to generate ideas. It is not unusual for participants to run out of ideas and have periods of silence during brainstorming. When this happens, don't stop the process. Encourage the group to combine, add, stretch, or manipulate the ideas that have already been listed.

Once you are confident that all the ideas have been generated, you can stop the idea generation phase. Participants can now ask questions, clarify, and eliminate redundant ideas on the list. Before evaluating the ideas, allow participants to take a break so that they can reflect on the ideas that they have generated. Then proceed to the idea evaluation phase. To maximize idea evaluation:

✓ *Pare down the list.* A brainstorming session can produce dozens of ideas, many of which are unworkable. Have the participants review the list of ideas. Which ones have the potential to solve the problem? Which ideas are not practical, but are interesting? Can some of the ideas be applied in a more practical way? After you pare down the list, you will have a small number of practical solutions. If your problem is relatively simple, this may be your last step.

✓ *Evaluate the remaining ideas.* Try using a decision matrix that utilizes your criteria and your short list of ideas. These matrices usually result in a numerical score. Remember that you do not have to choose the idea with the highest score; the scores simply give you additional information with which to make a decision. What is important is that you thoroughly consider all the ideas generated through brainstorming before making a final decision.

STAGES OF TEAM DEVELOPMENT

29

Phil Lohr and Patricia Steege

Phil Lohr *and* **Patricia Steege** *work as internal management development/organization development (MD/OD) consultants for Lockheed Martin's Enterprise Information Systems (EIS) Company, Bldg. 10, Room 1284D, PO Box 8048, Philadelphia, PA 19101. Phil (610-364-5338, philip j. lohr@den.mmc.com) authored the 1993 Best Practitioner Paper at the International Conference on Self-managed Work Teams. Prior to switching to the MD/OD profession, Phil was a program manager and software systems developer. Phil is also a master practitioner of neuro linguistic and time line therapy. Tricia (610-354-5739, tricia.steege@den.mmc.com) specializes in team and leadership development.*

OVERVIEW

Teams, like individuals, progress through various stages in their life cycles. Each stage of development holds its own unique relationships and demonstrated behaviors. The stages of team development must be understood by team members and leaders in order to recognize the signals that indicate normal team growth and development. Furthermore, the degree to which the leader interacts with the team varies from stage to stage. The combined efforts of leaders and team members to appropriately nurture the team will increase the probability of the team remaining intact and reaching its full potential.

Use the following handout to help identify which stage your team is at and what training interventions or leadership styles are most appropriate for maintaining it or progressing to a new stage.

STAGES OF TEAM DEVELOPMENT

Forming

The initial forming stage is the process of putting the structure of the team together. Team members enter with ambiguous feelings and attitudes. Conflict is avoided at all costs because of the need to be accepted into the group. Team members reflect not only on the tasks at handout, but also about each other.

Feelings and Thoughts	Observable Behaviors	Training and Resolution Needed	Leadership Style Required
Excitement; anticipation and optimism	Politeness	Team mission and purpose	**Directing**
	Guarded; watchful		Telling
Suspicion, fear, and anxiety about the job ahead	Sporadic participation	Team membership	Guiding
	First agreements	Team goals and objectives	Establishing
Pride in being chosen for the group	Attempts to define tasks and decisions on how it will be accomplished	Measurement and feedback	High task and low relationship involvement
Tentative attachment to team		Definition of roles and responsibilities	Manager makes decisions, tells group what to do, when, where, how, with whom to do it
Why am I here?	Attempts to establish acceptable group behavior	Team member expectations	
Why are they here?	Abstract discussions of concepts and issues	Team operational guidelines and procedures	Clear boundaries
What is expected of me?	Discussion of symptoms and problems not relevant to the task; difficulty in identifying relevant problems	Behavioral norms and values	One-way communication from leader to follower
How much influence will I have?		Effective meetings and facilitation	
How much am I willing to give?			
	Complaints about the organization		
	Decisions on what information needs to be gathered		
	Impatience with discussion		

This stage is characterized by competition and conflict among team members. In the process of organizing tasks, interpersonal conflicts will begin to surface. Leadership, structure, and power issues dominate. The team must grow from this testing mindset to one of problem solving in order to progress in its development.

Feelings and Thoughts	Observable Behaviors	Training and Resolution Needed	Leadership Style Required
Resistance to task	Arguing among members	Interpersonal relationships	**Coaching**
Fluctuations in attitude about the team	Defensiveness and competition	Identification of style differences	Provides guidance
What are the job-related risks and benefits of sharing information?	Polarizations and pecking orders in team	Effective listening	Clarifying
	Power struggles and clashes	Giving and receiving feedback	Persuading
			Explaining
What are the risks and benefits of being open or closed?	Lack of consensus-seeking behaviors	Conflict resolution	High directing and supporting behavior
Do I agree with the team's purpose?	Lack of progress	Leadership clarification	High task and high relationship involvement
Do I agree with the team's approach to accomplishing the task?	Establishing unrealistic goals	What position does the team take when people don't get along?	Leader consults but makes final decision
	Concern over excessive work	How should the team deal with violation of codes of conduct?	
How do I feel about my personal influence and freedom in the team?	Attacking the leader	What should we do it team gets stuck?	
	Confusion, loss of interest; opting out		
	Code-of-conduct violations		
	Poor attendance		
	Questioning wisdom of other members of the team		

In this stage, team members are breaking from paradigms of preconceived ideas and opinions. As the group develops cohesion, leadership is shared and team members are trusting one another. Interpersonal conflicts give way to sharing of feelings and creative thinking. The group operates in cohesion and members are glad to be a part of the team.

Feelings and Thoughts	Observable Behaviors	Training and Resolution Needed	Leadership Style Required
Sense of belonging to team	Procedures established and practiced in problem solving, leadership, resolving conflict	Decision making	**Supporting**
Personal accomplishments		Problem solving	Committing
I understand how I contribute effectively		Management coaching	Participating
I have freedom to be myself and express my ideas	Open, honest communication; practicing communication skills	Leadership skills	Encouraging
			Listening
I can trust my teammates and they trust me	Effective conflict resolution		Collaborating
Ability to express criticism constructively	Sincere attempts to achieve consensus decisions		High relationship and low task involvement
Acceptance of membership in the team	Free participation and risk taking		Minimal influence in decision making
Relief that it seems that everything is going to work out	Productive; steady progress		Promotes discussion
	Shared decision making		Asks for contributions from followers
	Develop routines		
	Unified mission and purpose		
	Focused problem solving		
	Sets and achieves task milestones		
	Members honoring code of conduct		
	Strong team identity		
	Healthy balance of power		

True interdependence is the mainstay of this stage of group development. The team is highly flexible as individuals adapt to meet the current needs of the team. There is high productivity in task and personal relationships. A team operating in this mode is unique and a value added to its organization.

Feelings and Thoughts	Observable Behaviors	Training and Resolution Needed	Leadership Style Required
High commitment	Constructive self-change	Coaching and counseling	**Delegation**
Trusting; friendships	Flexibility, versatility, and midcourse corrections	Measuring performance	Observing
Fun and excited		Customer focus	Monitoring
High personal development and creativity	Tries new way of doing things		Fulfilling
Involvement with team inspires the best in me	Excited participation, enthusiasm, and volunteerism		Low relationship and low task involvement
Understand other's strengths and weaknesses	Attachment to team, connectedness and unity		Provides little direction
	High level of mutual support		Leader sets goals; team accomplishes
	Humor		Low amounts of two-way communication needed
	Satisfaction at team's progress; celebrating successes		
	Expressions of pride in team's unique accomplishments		
	Ability to work through group problems; confronting with support		
	Ownership of results		
	True consensus decision making		
	Management and creative use of team's resources		
	Momentum maintained		
	Smooth task and process flow		
	Purpose and mission basis for action		
	Goal attainment		

REFERENCES

Hersey, P. 1984. *The Situational Leader.* New York: Warner Books, Inc.

Tuckman, B. W. and M. A. C. Jensen. 1977. Stages of small-group development revisted. *Group and Organization Studies,* December, 419–427.

TEN TEAM HATS

30

Cynthia Solomon

Cynthia Solomon, *Ph.D., is a technical program specialist for FERMCO, an environmental restoration company in Ohio (6469 Fountains Blvd., West Chester, OH 45069, 513-777-5435). Cindy had led or designed organizational and professional development projects for her employer, the health care industry, and professional organizations, and chairs the professional development committee of a chapter of the National Management Association. She authored* **TQM in Dietetics and Nutrition Services** *(Wolf Rinke Associates, 1993).*

OVERVIEW

A successful team relies on different members to provide various services to the whole group. Not everyone can do everything for the team, nor should everyone be expected to. There are some roles, often called *team hats,* that should be assumed by different teams members so that the group produces its deliverable at the level of quality its customer wants, on time and within budget. An effective team facilitator leads the newly formed group in a team-hats session in which the team defines what it needs from its members and negotiates and agrees on who will assume what roles.

Roles can be organized as leadership, task, and support positions. *Leadership positions* are those in which team members provide process management to the team and represent the team to the customer. *Task positions* are those in which team members are doing the work of the team that directly results in the deliverable to the customer. *Support services* are those activities that help the team to complete its work.

The following handout lists the typical roles and responsibilities that a team may require of some of its members. This list could be used by a team coach or facilitator to guide the team in a process to identify what roles they will need, define the scope of each role, and negotiate the assignment of responsibility of each role.

TEN TEAM HATS

Leadership Roles

1. *Team manager.* Ensures that the team is functioning effectively and efficiently. Principal line of accountability to the customer. Ensures that all required team roles are assigned and are completed as needed. Manages the plan.

2. *Facilitator.* Conducts the meeting according to the agenda. Ensures that the meeting proceeds within the time allotted. Ensures that all members of the team are able to contribute equally and that the team stays on task. May also be the team manager.

3. *Coach.* Provides advice to the individual team members and/or to the team as a whole so that they can manage their activity. May be a technical coach who gives advice on the technical issues surrounding the team's task.

Task Roles

4. *Historian.* Maintains or obtains historical records that are relevant to the team's task.

5. *Researcher.* Uses other resources, including libraries, technical experts, and other documents, to find and present supportive information to the team.

6. *Technical experts.* Use technical expertise to complete actions in the team's plan.

7. *Client contact.* Represents the team to the client to ensure that the client's needs for quality are known and to inform the client of progress made throughout the term of the team. Acts as point of contact to solicit periodic feedback and input from the client.

Support Roles

8. *Record manager.* Maintains all documentation of the team's activities. This may include agenda, minutes, action items, correspondence, reports, and other documentation. This role may also be combined with the secretarial duties.

9. *Secretary.* Maintains membership lists with phone numbers, mail address, e-mail address, and the like. Prepares the meeting agenda in advance of the meeting and distributes to members. Takes minutes and distributes. Prepares correspondence and distributes. May perform typing or word processing for the team (may delegate any of the these clerical tasks to an organizational secretary).

10. *Timekeeper.* Ensures that team meetings are paced so that all that is planned is covered. Alerts the team when time is running short so that the meeting can be ended with sufficient notice.

PRACTICAL GUIDES

In this section of *The 1996 McGraw-Hill Team and Organization Development Sourcebook,* you will find ten practical guides. These "how-to" guides are short articles containing useful ideas and guidelines for implementing a team or organizational initiative.

You will find advice about such initiatives as:

✓ Facilitating teams and managing conflict.

✓ Formulating an organization-wide vision and mission statement.

✓ Developing partnerships between teams.

✓ Implementing continuous quality improvement.

✓ Using criterion-referenced testing.

✓ Developing a healthy work environment.

✓ Introducing corporate culture into the hiring process.

Each guide contains step-by-step advice. Several have examples, illustrations, charts, and tables to enhance your understanding of the content. You will find that these guides are clearly organized and easy to read.

Four uses for the practical guides are suggested:

1. As guidelines for your own consulting, facilitating, and training interventions

2. As implementation advice to be shared with peers and people who report to you

3. As recommendations to senior management

4. As reading assignments in team building and organizational consultations and training programs

HOW TO FACILITATE PROCESS ENGINEERING TEAMS

Cathleen Hutchison

Cathleen Smith Hutchison *is managing partner of Conifer Consulting Group (PO Box 1147, Cedar Crest, NM 87008, 505-281-4496), a full-service human resource consulting firm specializing in managing corporate change, including change components such as culture change and reengineering. She is a past officer of the National Society for Performance and Instruction at national and chapter levels and of the International Board of Standards for Training, Performance, and Instruction.*

Organizations are increasingly using process engineering as a means of achieving organizational performance improvement. The method described in this guide is designed to minimize the time spent by cross-functional teams charged with the development of new processes and to maximize the effectiveness of those teams.

The purpose behind facilitating a process engineering team is twofold. First, the facilitator helps a team to develop work processes the way they *should* operate for present and future flexibility. The team develops *maps* of the process(es) as they *should* flow. Second, the facilitator helps the team to create several other products to prioritize and maximize the effectiveness of implementation of the engineered process(es). This guide will show you to accomplish this.

Equipment and Materials

There are four main methods to accomplish the facilitation of cross-functional process engineering teams. Each of the four methods ties to different sets of equipment and materials. Table 31.1 lists them with their associated positives and negatives.

The Facilitator's Role

If the organization is using any of the first three methods, a single facilitator is all that is required on the team. The facilitator should, however, focus solely on facilitating the group process and not be expected to also

Table 31.1.

Method (equipment and materials)	Associated Positives	Associated Negatives
Flip chart and markers	Inexpensive and readily available Can be easily transported	Difficult to make changes during the process. Process maps become messy very quickly as changes are recognized and captured. Usually must be recopied into another medium for permanence and distribution.
White board and markers or black board and chalk (subset is electronic white board)	Inexpensive and readily available Changes can be made as they are recognized during the process mapping	Must be recopied into another medium for permanence, distribution and transportability (this is not necessary with the electronic white board).
Post-it™ notes on butcher paper on walls	Inexpensive and easy to acquire Changes can be made as they are recognized during the process mapping.	Major process mapping projects may need to be planned for in advance in order to have sufficient supplies on hand. Must be recopied into another medium for permanence, distribution, and transportability.
Computer-supported video projection	Changes can be made as they are recognized during the process mapping Printouts can provide easy take-aways during and at completion of the process mapping	Expensive equipment that is not readily available in all organizations: ✓ Video projector and screen ✓ Computer, preferably with a color monitor or screen ✓ Printer, preferably with color printout ✓ Flow chart software, such as Corel Flow or ABC Flowchart

be a participating member of the process engineering team. It is difficult for a single individual to both (1) manage the group process and (2) contribute content for the team. One or both activities generally suffer.

The facilitator (1) manages the group process, (2) keeps participants focused on the task, and (3) guides the process engineering team to create their outputs.

The individual in the facilitator role should be someone whom all process engineering team members view as neutral. The team needs to eliminate current barriers to moving forward. Anyone viewed as a part of the barrier or as having a "political axe to grind" could inhibit the efforts of the team. For this reason, it is usually preferable to have a facilitator who is external to the organization conducting the process engineering. However, a facilitator from another division, subsidiary, or part of the organization can also accomplish this task.

If the organization is using the fourth method, computer-supported video projection, it is best to have a skilled person devoted to capturing the flow chart information. He or she can move process steps around the screen as changes are made. There should be one individual whose sole task it is to manage this activity. This individual should not be expected or required to either facilitate or contribute content to the process engineering team.

Composing Process Engineering Teams

The members of the process engineering team should be chosen by the organization to represent all functions and areas that are (or will be) involved in the performance of the process(es) to be engineered and that use the outputs of the process(es) to be engineered. Sometimes it is also useful to include individuals skilled at lateral thinking who have *no* vested interest in the process.

Ideally, there will be between 6 and 12 members on the team. They should be individuals who are willing to speak up in a group and are knowledgeable of as much of the work process(es) and its outputs as possible. As with the facilitator, it is best if the participants can be viewed as relatively neutral to the process. This may be difficult, since all the participants are invested in the process and/or its outputs or they would not be considered for selection. The facilitator therefore must be sensitive to any issues around individual process engineering team members.

Timing

Unfortunately, the time involved cannot be pinpointed accurately because it varies quite a bit from project to project. Clearly, a big project and/or one with many processes to be analyzed will require the greatest investment in time. However, the following information provides estimates and guidelines to help to determine the time necessary to engage in a process engineering exercise.

1. *Preparation time.* Preparation involves identifying the team, ensuring that the facilitator is familiar with any relevant interpersonal and political issues related to the process engineering team or relevant historical or contextual issues, gathering the materials and equipment, and arranging site and timing logistics for the meeting. This could include travel and accommodations for participants coming from other corporate locations.

   The time needed depends on the level of familiarity the facilitator has with the organization and the breadth of scope of the area targeted for process engineering. An external facilitator having no familiarity with the organization preparing to engineer processes across the organization would plan for 1- to 2-hour interviews with 10 to 12 key individuals at multiple levels within the organization. These interviews focus on how the organization operates now and the problems that exist or are causing the need for the process engineering project at this time. Tours of the worksite(s) can also be very helpful to the facilitator, particularly in manufacturing settings.

2. *Process engineering time.* This includes only the time when the cross-functional process engineering team is meeting to develop the processes. Most targeted areas can be completed in five days or less, at least at a general overview level. Typically, lower-level processes and/or procedures will need to be developed as well. The larger the scope of the original targeted area, the more likely there will be a need for elaboration or additional detail. There will also be time involved in analyzing implications for other areas, functions, and processes.

3. *Follow-up time.* The amount of time needed will vary greatly with the scope of the project. Factors that can affect the time include review by others involved, development of lower-level subprocesses or procedures where necessary, communication of processes and procedures throughout the organization, analysis of implications for other areas, and clarification and validation of metrics.

4. *Implementation time.* The amount of time needed will vary greatly with the scope of the project. Factors that can affect the time required include development of implementation plan, analysis of implications for other areas, identification of process champions, communication of implementation plan and timetable, development of any needed forms, software support, policies, and so on.

Process Engineering Steps

The following list of steps includes not only those that are undertaken during the actual process engineering sessions (steps 4 through 17), but also steps that occur prior and subsequent to the session. This will help the organization fit these sessions into a sequence of events that will result in the implementation of effective and efficient processes operating as they should operate. Steps 4 through 17 are identified in smaller increments and more detail than those preceding or following them. These steps are the focus of this guide.

Prior to the Process Engineering Session

1. *Identify the target areas to be engineered.* In some cases, this is a specific process or procedure from the beginning. In most cases, however, it is a larger work area such as customer service, cargo transshipment, or accounts payable. Each of these targets is actually comprised of several processes, subprocesses, and procedures. As the target is being identified, the organization should take into consideration how and where this area interfaces with the rest of the organization.

2. *Identify related historical and contextual issues.* Before undertaking process engineering projects, the level of readiness of the organization must be determined. Issues that are related to readiness include any recent reorganizations or major initiatives, the morale of the organization, the employees' receptivity to major changes, and other historical and contextual events within the organization.

3. *Identify the teams.* Refer to the team composition descriptions earlier in this guide. The organization identifies those individuals who will be part of the facilitation team and the process engineering team. It may also be useful to identify other experts who may be called on from time to time to share information and specific expertise with the process engineering team.

During the Process Engineering Session

4. *Convene and introduce the team.* Depending on the size of the organization, individuals may not know people from other functions or areas. Members should identify themselves by name, function, length of service, relationship to the targeted area, or any other useful information relevant to engineering processes for the targeted area.

5. *State the purpose of process engineering.* The facilitator describes what the organization's expectations are for the activity, including the products from the activity and the longer-term outcomes, and answers any questions from the participants.

6. *Establish ground rules for operation (what and how).* The facilitator describes what will be done throughout the time frame and facilitates the group to develop a set of operational ground rules, such as the following:

   ✓ Full participation by all team members

   ✓ Openness and candor throughout

   ✓ No personal attacks

   ✓ Wear a "big picture" hat to view things from the corporate perspective

   ✓ No personal agendas

   ✓ Breaks, phone messages, and the like

7. *Define the targeted area, process, or group of processes to be mapped.* The facilitator describes the targeted area as it has been defined by the organization. This may include limits and boundaries of what areas will and will not be included in the process engineering session. This definition can be modified, expanded, or limited based on the knowledge and expertise of the group. The group participants may have a better idea of interrelated areas, functions, and processes than those who created the initial definition of the targeted area. The process engineering team agrees on a working definition of its targeted area and what falls inside and outside the boundaries.

8. *Identify the outcomes of efficient process(es) in the target area.* The facilitator helps the group to expand their thinking by brainstorming outcomes for the organization if the processes in the targeted area were functioning efficiently and effectively. These outcomes may reflect technical, managerial, or cultural outcomes. A list of outcomes is created. The list is then analyzed and related outcomes are grouped into categories to be addressed in the next step. Positive outcomes are addressed by creating spider diagrams. Negative outcomes are addressed by listing them as barriers.

9. *Develop a spider diagram of the elements required to produce an outcome or group of outcomes.* The facilitator asks the group to focus on the selected outcome. The identified outcome is written in the center of the page or board, depending on the materials and equipment being used. The facilitator then asks participants what must be in place for the desired outcome to be reached. As each element is identified, it is linked to the central outcome, like the legs of a spider (see Figure 31.1).

    Some questions that can be used to elicit a lower level of related elements are the following:

    ✓ What are some elements that are necessary to achieve this outcome?

    ✓ What do we need to have in place to reach this outcome?

    ✓ What elements are behind this?

This process is repeated for each element identified at the first level. The facilitator asks what must be in place for this element to occur. Lower-level elements are linked to first-level elements in the same manner. This continues until all outcomes (considered important by the process engineering team) have been addressed.

This process creates one or more expanding, multilevel spider diagrams (see Figure 31.2). To maintain clarity in the diagram, it is helpful to use a different shaped symbol and/or color for each *level* of elements that is identified. These elements can be either resources and technology that must be in place, management and/or employee practices that must be adhered to, or events that must occur.

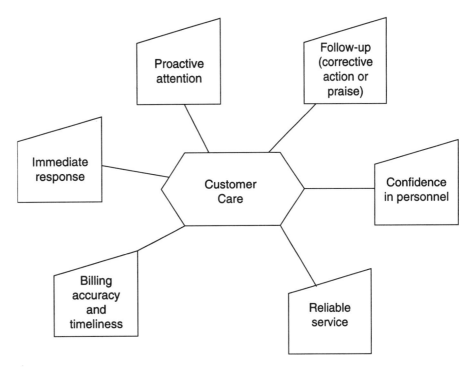

Figure 31.1. Customer Care.

10. *Select a process to map.* In most cases no prioritization is necessary. All processes will be addressed during the process engineering session. However, if time is limited and/or the targeted area is quite broad, the group may wish to develop prioritization criteria and select the process(es) based on these criteria.

11. *Develop the process map.* The group can map the process by starting at either end. When starting at the beginning of the process, the facilitator asks the group to determine "what should be" the initiating event for the process to reach desired outcome or results. This event is recorded as the first step in the process map. The facilitator asks what "should" happen next, and each step in the process is recorded until the process has been completed as it "should" be performed.

    When starting at the end of the process, the facilitator asks the group to begin with the outcome and determine "what should be" the last step prior to reaching that outcome. This event is recorded as the last step in the process map. The facilitator then asks what "should" happen just prior to that, and each step in the process is recorded until the initiating event is reached. Figure 31.3 is an example of a process map.

    Note: There are standard conventions for diagraming process steps. Some groups may wish to use these standard conventions. At the same time, however, it may help to move the group out of conventional thinking if other symbols are used in the process. In either event, a set of symbol conventions should be used through-

166

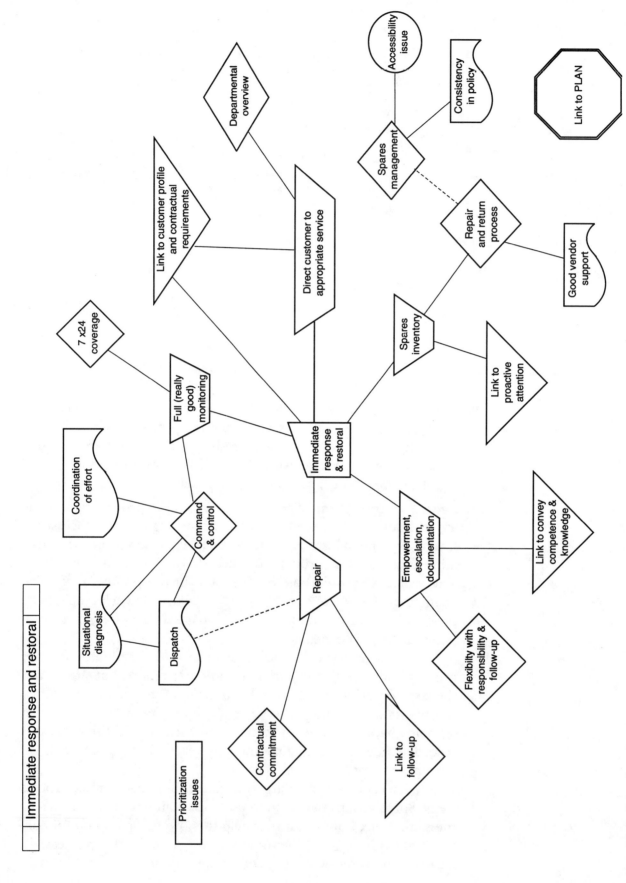

Figure 31.2. Immediate Response and Restoral.

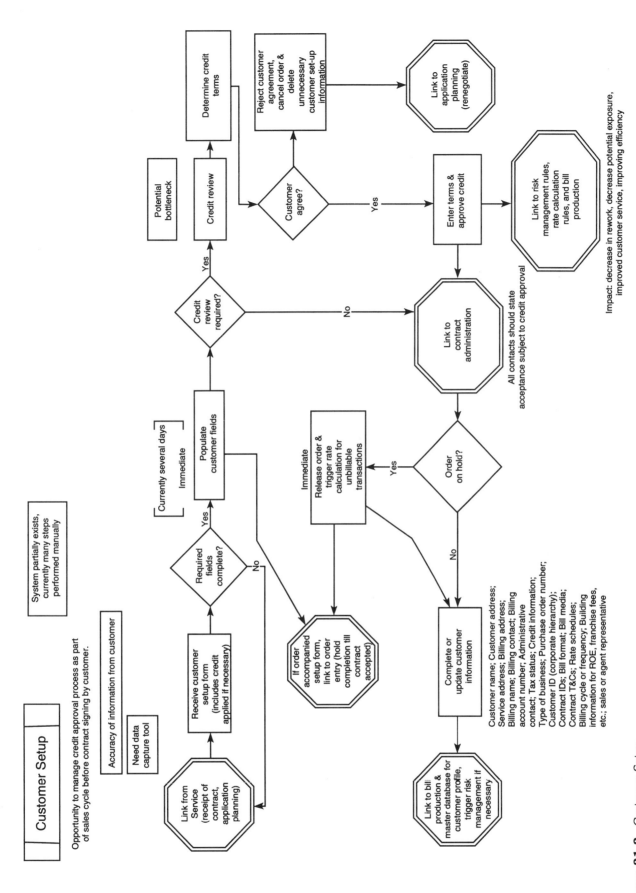

Figure 31.3. Customer Setup

out a map or series of maps so that process steps are readily identified, as are decision boxes and linkages to other mapped processes. If color capabilities are available, it is also helpful to use a different color for each type of symbol. If multiple teams are meeting, conventions should be standard across all teams.

One of the main tasks for the facilitator is to keep the participants focused on what should happen at a strategic level for the good of the overall organization.

✓ Many participants become bogged down in "That's the way we've always done it, so that's the way it must be" thinking.

✓ Others find it difficult to move beyond their own parochial viewpoints to see what is best for the organization, especially if it does not appear best for their function or area.

The team may find it useful to invite additional content experts into the sessions to brief them on aspects of the process with which they are not familiar.

12. *Test the process map.* The facilitator questions the process engineering team regarding the viability of the process as mapped to most effectively deliver the positive outcomes expected by the organization. This step can be conducted concurrently with or subsequent to the completion of the process map. Some of the questions asked are as follows:

✓ Why should we do it this way?

✓ Why should we *not* do it another way?

✓ Will this process provide flexibility for growth and change in the future?

✓ Who cares that this step is completed? Why?

✓ Who uses the output of this step? What do they use it for and how do they use it? Will this give them what they need in a way that they can easily use it?

✓ What are the consequences of not doing this step?

✓ What are the consequences of doing this step a different way?

✓ In a perfect world, how would this happen?

13. *Identify barriers to the process being performed as mapped.* Barriers can be technology that is not available or not yet in place, information that is not available, equipment and/or resource limitations, management or employee practices, systems or policies that run counter to the desired outcome, related outcomes that run counter to the overall desired outcomes, or organizational values and beliefs that inhibit the ability of the organization to move toward the desired processes (see Figure 31.3).

14. *Determine metrics where appropriate.* Identify where measurement of time, quantity, and/or quality would be useful. The group may also

be able to provide a best guess of "how many should be accomplished to what standard in what timeframe by how many" (see Figure 31.3).

15. *Identify the impact on the organization of the process being performed as mapped.* The facilitator assists the process engineering team to provide a best guess of the potential impact that the engineered processes will have on the organization. These impacts can be compared and used to prioritize implementation (see Figure 31.3).

16. *Repeat until all processes have been mapped.* Repeat steps 10 through 15 until either all processes deemed to be important by the process engineering team are mapped or the available time has elapsed.

17. *Identify all interconnections of the processes.* Identify how the processes that have been mapped link to each other: Where do they flow from one process into another? Where do they bump up against another? Where do they branch off into others depending on conditions? (See Figure 31.3.)

Following the Process Engineering Session

18. *Prioritize processes for implementation.* The organization prioritizes the processes according to its own criteria. Some criteria that might be used are listed next:

   ✓ *The potential impact on the organization.* Generally, most organizations can reference the following prioritization list:

   > The highest priority is processes that have impact visible to the customer.

   > The second highest priority is to improve processes that have impact across the entire organization.

   > The next highest priority is to improve processes that affect two or more cross-functional work groups.

   > The lowest priority is to improve processes that affect solely an intact work group

   ✓ *The level of dependencies of the process.* Stand-alone processes are simpler and quicker to implement than processes interwoven with many other processes or dependent on other events to occur for their implementation. Work processes that can be improved in isolation might be better targets than processes that have others leading up to them or resulting from them. Sometimes these dependencies can be subtle. A company can buy a technology solution, but if the rest of the organization is not poised to incorporate the technology, the company may be wasting resources.

   ✓ *Potential gains in time, cost, and effort.* Some processes will significantly reduce the time, resource demand, cost, and/or effort involved in accomplishing the task(s). There may be a significant payoff in reduced cycle time, reduced resource demand, or improved quality or flexibility.

  ✓ *Potential for automation.* Automation may be able to replace work currently done by personnel, freeing them for other more valuable tasks. *Caution:* Don't just automate existing processes. You may be continuing inefficiencies.

19. *Identify process owners.* Process owners should ideally be in positions of responsibility and accountability for the output of their work. Process owners are charged with removing barriers to the implementation of the process and with monitoring and measuring the impact on the organization. The process owner must have a systems view of the process and work toward optimization for the organization rather than for any single function or area.

20. *Develop subprocesses and procedures where needed.* As appropriate, individuals, functional teams, or cross-functional teams work to provide more detail in subprocesses and procedures where they are needed. To accomplish this, many of the steps in this method may be repeated to deal with a lower level of detail.

21. *Develop implementation plan.* The organization reviews the results of the process engineering team and any other process or procedure development activities. This includes the process maps, the spider diagrams, the list of barriers, the list of metrics, and the list of relative impacts on the organization. This information is used to identify issues that should be part of the implementation plan, both procedural and cultural, to determine the scope of the implementation and to prioritize the activities for implementation.

22. *Implement.* The organization carries out the implementation plan.

Products and/or Deliverables

The products of the process engineering sessions will be as follows:

  ✓ *A list of process outcomes expected.* This is a list of outcomes that the organization should expect to occur when the targeted area is functioning as it should with the new effective and efficient processes and procedures.

  ✓ *Spider diagrams identifying the elements that must be in place for effective implementation (technical, managerial, and cultural elements).* This is a diagram specifying elements that have been identified as necessary for effective implementation of the processes as they should be, but which may or may not be in place in reality. This diagram of elements can be used to develop the implementation plan (see Figure 31.2).

  ✓ *Process maps.* These diagrams depict the way processes in the targeted area should flow for maximum effectiveness and efficiency in the future. They provide a road map for the implementation plan. They may provide process flow information at various levels of detail and they will show the interrelationships of processes (see Figure 31.3).

✓ *A list of barriers to implementation.* This list describes elements in the current organization that will inhibit easy implementation of the processes as they should flow. The list will be developed to be process-specific. Therefore, a matrix can be developed to identify how broadly a single barrier affects a number of processes in the targeted area. This matrix can be used to prioritize steps in the implementation process (see Table 31.2).

✓ *A list of metrics.* This list identifies steps in the process(es) where measurement would provide useful information for the organization. In addition, it identifies appropriate standards for the measurements.

✓ *A list of relative impacts on the organization.* This list identifies the amount and types of impacts the organization should realize from implementation of the process(es). This information can be used for prioritization of implementation.

REFERENCE

Hutchison, Cathleen. 1994. "A process for reengineering processes," an unpublished working paper available by writing Conifer Consulting Group, 12953 Lori Drive, Conifer, Colorado, 80433, or by calling 303-838-1668.

Table 31.2.

	Getting the order	Generate the order	Install	Routine maintenance	Spares management	Return and repair	Applications planning	Contract administration	Process improvement	Customer setup	Format	Bill production	Cash applications	Tax remittance	Revenue accounting	Inquiry management	Risk management	Market planning	New product	Budget development	Purchasing	Accounts payable
Process does not exist				X	X	X		X	X		X					X	X	X				
Inconsistent use of product code												X										
Incorrect data entry												X										
Manual process										X			X	X	X	X						X
Inadequate control systems													X									
Inadequate procedures													X									X
Incomplete or inaccurate data										X					X		X			X	X	
Inadequate systems		X	X				X				X	X										X
Approval process		X											X							X	X	X
Inadequate documentation	X		X		X		X	X								X						X
Inadequate coordination	X	X	X			X	X	X	X							X	X	X	X			
Vendor relations		X	X		X	X																
Knowledge and skills	X					X	X									X		X	X			
Forecasting							X											X				
Commitment of resources				X	X	X																

HOW TO INCLUDE EVERYONE IN DEVELOPING A MISSION STATEMENT

Jeanne Baer

Jeanne Baer *is president of Creative Training Solutions (1649 South 21st Street, Lincoln, NE 68502, 800-410-3178, jbaer@grex.cyberspace.org). The company provides training, facilitation, and program design services to clients as diverse as Chrysler, Burlington Northern, IDS, the International Festivals Association, and the Travel Industry Association of America. She teaches at Southeast Community College, writes for* **Training Media Review,** *and is a past president of the Lincoln, Nebraska, chapter of the American Society for Training and Development.*

Traditionally, a mission statement is composed by a few people near the top of the organization. This guide explains how to facilitate a session in which a mission statement can be crafted by a much larger group of employees at all levels.

A clear mission statement provides a framework for its members to make decisions, solve problems, and chart future direction. It is the foundation for goals, strategies, and even policies that will guide the organization's day-to-day operations. If the mission is inspiring and easily understood, it is more likely to be embraced by its employees or members. And if those in the organization have a hand in composing it themselves, the buy-in will be almost guaranteed. Other benefits of involving as many people as possible in the process are that the organization hears diverse ideas and that people can air and resolve differences that they have about the organization's mission.

Preparing for the Session

Gather plenty of medium- to large-point dark-colored felt-tip pens, ideally one for every participant. Also gather material to write on that will stick to another surface. Large removable labels, Post-it™ notes, or small static-cling-type plastic sheets, Jotz, by Keith Clark work well. If you do not have a large wall available (to stick these materials onto), then have flip charts on three to five easels at the front of the room.

You may also want to prepare some audiovisual aids to illustrate the lecture points you will be making about the purpose for and elements of mission statements.

1. Begin the process by calling together no more than 50 employees from the organization. (If you have more people than this, conduct additional sessions and combine people's opinions.) Welcome them and introduce them to the concept of a mission statement.

2. Describe the purpose of a mission statement: *to outline a common set of goals and beliefs for an organization.* It paints the "big picture" that lets everyone in the organization know why the organization exists and where it is going. It gives employees and customers a sense that there are clear guiding principles.

3. Share with them some mission statements that you feel are particularly good or some from organizations similar to theirs. For instance, the Disney mission statement is "We create happiness by providing the finest in entertainment for people of all ages, everywhere." Ritz-Carlton's is "We are ladies and gentlemen, serving ladies and gentlemen." The mission statement for the American Society for Training and Development is "We provide leadership to individuals, organizations, and society to achieve work-related competence, performance, and fulfillment."

4. Point out the elements commonly included in a mission statement:
   ✓ What business the organization is really in
   ✓ What services it really provides
   ✓ The organization's special approach to the marketplace
   ✓ The strengths of the organization
   ✓ What it wants to accomplish

   Also, explain that the mission statement is often accompanied by a declaration and affirmation of the core values or principles that should guide planning, day-to-day decisions, and activities.

5. Point out how the mission statements that you have used as examples contain these elements. For instance, the Disney mission is to "create happiness" not to "run theme parks and make movies and money."

6. Invite people to consider, on an individual basis, what words or concepts come to mind when they think of their organization and these elements. Stress the importance of looking at the "forest," rather than getting hung up on individual "trees." You might say, "Putting aside exactly what you do on a day-to-day basis for a moment (trees), consider how we serve both internal and external customers. What would that service look like to each other and to outsiders in an ideal world? What are some of the words that pop into your head?" Have participants jot down these words or phrases in large letters, each on a separate Post-it™ note.

7. When they have finished thinking and writing a few words, ask participants to share these with the larger group by shouting out a word

and handing it to a volunteer, who will bring it forward and attach it to the wall or onto a flip chart. People should only call out one of their words at a time versus reading their whole list at once. People should be encouraged to keep thinking as they hear other's words and feel free to continue to add new words. Meanwhile, the facilitator should be thinking about any natural categories of words and phrases that might be taking shape.

8. Once people have volunteered all the words or phrases that they care to, start sorting. The facilitator, with permission from the group, can first look for any synonyms and put them together. Then the facilitator and participants should suggest the main categories or themes that they observe and peel off and reattach the suggested words and phrases so that those that speak to the same issues are together.

Composing the Actual Statement

1. Once this sorting has taken place and a general consensus has emerged about what the mission should "feel" like, the most creative part of the process has ended. Now ask the group's permission to proceed with writing the exact statement, for its later approval. Obtain no more than five (three would be best) volunteers to craft the statement based on what has already been suggested. This large group is now adjourned.

2. The three to five volunteers now write a statement that incorporates the spirit of what has been suggested by all in the room. When they are finished, it is important that all feel that they have been a part of the approval process. At another group meeting, the statement can be revealed. You, as the facilitator, or someone from the statement committee can point out how the group assimilated the words, phrases, and spirit suggested by employees into this statement. If there are no major problems with it, it can then be ratified.

Other Options

1. If your group is large enough to intimidate timid members, you might have them share some of these concepts in a small group, before shouting them out to the larger group.

2. If your total number of employees is large, you should divide it into groups no larger than 50 and run several sessions. Only one group of three to five should draft the exact statement, which should blend the opinions of all groups.

3. If time is short, you can just solicit words and phrases from participants but leave the categorizing to the smaller committee.

4. The smaller committee can also write a list of values or guiding principles that are more specific statements of the kinds of behavior that support the mission statement. A committee spokesperson can then point out how employees' words and phrases were incorporated into

these statements. The values can usually be approved and ratified at the same time that the mission statement is.

5. If reconvening the original brainstorming group(s) is unwieldy, the proposed mission statement could be distributed by memo to all employees. The memo should thank all for their input and describe briefly how the spirit of their remarks was translated into the proposed statement. The memo might offer that if the reader objects to the statement, she or he should voice opinions by X date; otherwise the statement will be considered approved and will go into use on X date.

6. The small group that crafts the mission could decide to propose two statements for consideration. Giving a choice might help to involve everyone again as key players in the decision process.

HOW TO JUMP START YOUR TEAM'S CREATIVITY

33

Bryan Mattimore

Bryan W. Mattimore, *is president of The Mattimore Group (One Landmark Square, Stamford, CT 06901, 203-359-1801), an innovation training and creative problem-solving consulting firm. He is the author of the book on applied creativity,* **99% Inspiration: Tips, Tales and Techniques to Liberate Your Business Creativity** *(AMACOM, 1994), as well a contributing editor to* **SUCCESS** *magazine. Bryan facilitates over 75 ideation sessions per year and is a popular keynote speaker.*

The U.S. government has asked you to run process reengineering sessions. A major phone company is looking for your assistance on a quality improvement project. A softdrink manufacturer has asked your help in developing new product names. What do these three situations have in common? They are all real-life opportunities for a creativity consultant. Read the following first-person account of a consultant who facilitates ideation sessions to learn how you too can jump start a team's creativity and supercharge a team's productivity.

I would like you to imagine that you have just enrolled yourself in comedy training school. Pretend that there are three tracks or courses of study that you can major in: comedy writing, stand-up comedy, or improvisational comedy performing. Which would you choose?

I was quite surprised—and encouraged—that when I posed just such a question to a group of 60 trainers and consultants in New York City close to 90% said that they would take improvisational comedy performing. For me, the three comedy tracks represent the three key skills in innovation training and facilitation: course design (comedy writing), training (stand-up comedy, that is, delivering already created material), and ideation facilitation (improvisation). The interest in the improvisational track says to me that trainers and consultants are looking to expand their skills beyond merely the design and delivery of prepackaged programs into the potentially more dynamic—and, frankly, riskier—business of facilitating ideation sessions. And so what follows are some of the tricks I have either invented or adapted over the last 15 years to help me to jump start team creativity.

A good way to make sure that your ideation session hits the ground running is to prepare a briefing document. As its name implies, a *briefing document* informs all the session participants, generally a week or so in advance of the actual session, about the problem(s) the group is trying to solve.

The briefing document should also include creative exercises, specific to the problem, that encourage the participants to start getting ideas. For example, suppose that you wanted to brainstorm more effective ways to communicate with your customers. Your briefing document might include exercises that forced group members to think about the nature of communication: What are the advantages of using smoke signals versus a telephone? If all your employees were telepathic, how might this help business? What if they could not hear, or see, or speak?

Or suppose that you wanted to invent a line of new kitchen implements. Your briefing document might include a list of kitchen activities, for example, dicing, slicing, shredding, and boiling, and the problems associated with these activities (cut or burnt fingers). The document might also ask the participants for preliminary new-product ideas.

In one session I facilitated to create new-product ideas for a maker of polyurethane foam, we included in our briefing document an imaginary tour of the kitchen, dining room, bedroom, living room, garage, tool shop, and gardener's shed. By helping the participants to visualize these rooms and locations and by providing lists of specific objects or things they might see when they got there, we helped them to trigger possible new-product ideas and uses for the urethane foam. One participant said the briefing document helped him to "see an ugly, brown television cord plugged into a living room wall. It made me wonder if we could create a line of designer polyurethane covers for electrical cords to make them look prettier to go with the room better. Maybe they could be insulated to help prevent fires as well?"

Beyond the sheer number of good (and sometimes great) ideas that your participants will bring to the session, the briefing document will help prime their subconscious minds so that, when they do attend the actual session, they will be that much more likely to contribute a truly great idea.

Setting the Mood: Props, Props, Props

Science fiction writer Ray Bradbury wrote in a room filled with everything from toy dinosaurs to a globe, a bag of marbles to a model of the space shuttle. He used these props to help him get ideas for stories—and trigger creative connections among story elements that he otherwise might not make. Why not do the same for your ideation session?

If you are trying to invent an environmentally safe new form of packaging, why not fill the brainstorming room with exotic plants and play new-age background music? If you are looking for futuristic banking concepts, why not put up pictures of the Starship Enterprise?

Do these kind of props really help the creative process? They certainly do. When new-product consultant Steve Kaye was asked to help executives of the Life Savers Company invent new flavors, he filled the room with hundreds of flavors ideas: from a list of 75+ Baskin & Robbins flavors, to actual samples of exotic fruits (kiwi's, kumquats, and the like) to a wide variety of perfume fragrances and scents. Life Savers highly successful Fruit Juicers line came out of that session.

When Doug Hall, former in-house inventor for Procter & Gamble, was trying to invent a new line of cake products for P & G's Duncan Hines division, he filled the room with everything he could imagine to make the session more stimulating and fun. Among his props were greeting cards, which ultimately triggered the idea for Duncan Hines's line of Pantastic Party Cakes. Among the party cake themes, complete with specially molded pans and cardboard decorations, are Garfield, Kermit, and Miss Piggy cakes.

Selecting Your Ideation Team: Don't Forget to …

The single most important question you can ask yourself about the makeup of your ideation team is "Who will be the most senior member or boss in the group, and what is his or her relationship with the other participants?" Unless you have a truly superior manager, someone who really does believe in empowering the people that work for him or her, you may be in for a less than stellar session if the senior manager is included. If the relationship between the boss and his or her co-workers is about power, and therefore fear, you will not see a great deal of creative risk taking among the other members of the group. And without risk taking, you have little hope of getting a truly original idea.

A case in point is a series of three creativity training and ideation sessions for the Los Angeles manufacturing plant of an international packaged goods marketer. In all three sessions we had a wide range of ethnically diverse participants from all levels and departments within the company, as well as a senior manager. Sessions 1 and 3 were two of the best sessions I have ever conducted. We generated several great ideas and, without exception, the group participants greatly appreciated the creativity training. Credit for the success of these sessions was due, in no small part, to the genuine desire of the two senior managers to empower their employees.

And then there was session 2. Ratings in this session were the lowest we had ever gotten, averaging below 5 on the possible 10-point scale (the two other sessions averaged 9.4). What could account for such widely divergent ratings when all three sessions had the same basic design and facilitator?

Feelings of fear, versus a desire to empower, were the difference. Session 2 had an insecure and, in my opinion, bitter and unhappy boss in charge. Some of his power-play ploys were subtle and, at other times, blatantly aggressive attacks. Those brave souls that did speak up were quickly beaten down despite my attempts to defend them, and the others in the group quickly learned that the safest thing to do was to just keep quiet. The irony was that by the end of the day—after relentless attempts on my part to build some level of trust and creative risk taking—the manager finally did start to come around. When we got past his insecurities (masked by an aura of presumed self-confidence), he actually proved himself to be quite talented and creative. Even some of the group began catch the spirit and make valuable contributions. It was still a shame though that we had to waste most of the day dealing with this manager's insecurities before we could make some progress.

By the way, if you are interested in how one goes about trying to build some level of trust in this kind of situation, my approach has always been to enlist the problem person as a kind of ally. Recognizing that the problem person's fears and insecurities often translate to a need to be in control, I often let them do just that. I ask them for advice on how to proceed in facilitating the session, "since this is obviously a more difficult assignment than we had previously thought." With this tack, all but the most cynical of people or bosses will quickly become the facilitator's ally and make all kinds of suggestions, often surprisingly good ones, on how best to proceed.

It's Show Time: Breaking the Ice

It is 8:30 A.M. on the day of the ideation session. In front of you are a dozen co-workers and/or clients. Everyone has had coffee and doughnutd, and all eyes are upon you, the facilitator and fearless leader of this newest effort into the unknown. As you begin talking about the day, the goals, the expectations, and the logistics, you are surprised to discover that you have an uneasy feeling developing in the pit of your stomach. You are sensing that many of the people in your session don't necessarily want to be there. Some seem to be skeptical, some bored, others seem to be just plain afraid of this whole "creativity" thing. Worse yet, some participants don't seem to particularly like or trust the other people in the room. So what do you do?

How can you (1) help to make the people feel comfortable and even begin to trust one another, (2) take the "creative pressure" off them, (3) show them it is okay to fail, in fact critical to the creative process that they do fail, and (4) if possible, get them laughing or at least smiling? And do all this in 10 minutes or less with a warm-up exercise?

The icebreaker exercise I invented called *Those Crazy Inventors* does indeed build trust, champion failure, relieve performance anxiety, and get everyone laughing. *Those Crazy Inventors* is a multiple-choice test in which the goal is to guess which of the three equally absurd choices is actually true. Here are three examples:

1. As part of his grooming regimen, Henry Ford would
   a. add particles of sand to his toothpaste to increase its abrasive tartar-removing qualities.
   b. dye his hair with rusty water.
   c. keep the balls of his feet soft by applying a coating of his own saliva to them nightly.

2. George Eastman, inventor of the Kodak camera,
   a. was a supporter of the 13-month calendar.
   b. took a photograph of himself every day from age 31 to 72.
   c. invented a camera that, when swallowed by cows, took pictures of each of their four stomachs.

3. Milkman Gail Borden
   a. had his tomb built in the shape of a condensed-milk can.
   b. tried to sell condensed cow's blood as an ingredient in a salad dressing.
   c. filled a public pool with milk to promote the idea that milk baths were good for the skin.

The correct answers are (1) b; (2) a; (3) a. What is great about this exercise is that it is quick and fun and, because of the trivia element, interesting to most people. Most importantly though, everyone has to risk being a little foolish by voting for one of these obviously ridiculous choices. Since there is no way to reason out the correct answer, a creative risk has to be taken. And creative risk taking is what a successful ideation session is all about. After all, if someone as successful and creative as Henry Ford or George Eastman was willing to risk such a seemingly absurd act or thought as the one above, why can't you? Invariably, after trying this exercise, everyone in the room begins to take themselves a little less seriously, which, of course, can dramatically add to the success of any ideation session.

Ice Breaker 2: When You Wish upon a Star ...

If you could have any job, what would it be? U.S. senator? Rock star? Forest ranger? As a trade show promotion for a large personnel firm, I once created a "Fantasy Occupation" survey and contest. Among the 596 conference attendees that entered the contest, do you know what the single most mentioned fantasy occupation was? I was surprised to discover that among these ostensibly conservative businesspeople the number one fantasy job was *secret agent!* Other top choices, in order of preference, included (2) actor, (3) U.S. senator, (4) rock star, (5) artist, (6) astronaut, (7) safari guide, (8) comedian, (9) inventor, (10) professional athlete, (11) novelist, and (12) chef.

The tremendous interest in our trade show promotion, coupled with the successful follow-up media coverage, confirmed something I suspected all along—people like to fantasize about having what other people have and doing what other people do. It can be a powerful human motivator. It can be a lot of fun. It can also be a great ideation-session icebreaker.

By having your group members imagine a fantasy occupation, you can quickly help them to get out of the limitations associated with their current occupations and into a world of infinite possibilities. It also allows each group member to get to know a facet of their co-workers' personalities that they probably had never before considered. The exercise helps to build team identity and trust because each person is confiding in the group something quite personal about themselves.

Another benefit of the fantasy occupation exercise, from the consultant's point of view, is that it gives him or her an insight—very quickly—into the mindsets, interests, motivations, and potentially unique capabilities of each group member. If someone's fantasy occupation is to be a college professor of philosophy, they can be relied on to provide ideas and insights in the session that are quite different from someone who would like to manage the girl's Olympic basketball team.

Finally, the fantasy occupation technique sets the stage for three of the most powerful idea generation techniques I often use in the course of a day-long ideation session: role playing, excursions, and the wish technique.

Of Role Playing, Excursions, and Wishing

In *role playing*, you simply pretend that you are someone else. Then you ask this "person" inside you for his or her ideas. It is amazing, but the human mind really can imagine how someone else might think about, or even solve, a problem that maybe the individual cannot solve. We can hear what "they" have to say about it and be the beneficiary of their advice. It is as if their voices live inside us, just waiting to be asked what "they" think. It is a simple, profound, and remarkably powerful technique, one that you can use either alone or with groups.

Often, when I use the role-playing technique in ideation sessions, I pass out identity cards with a picture and short biography of the role each person is to adopt. Some of my identity cards include photographers Mathew Brady and Ansel Adams, Florence Nightingale, Frank Lloyd Wright, Abraham Lincoln, Ben Franklin, Walt Disney, Will Rogers, Thomas Edison, Dr. Suess (Theodor Geisel), and Madame Tussaud (of wax museum fame). Then I simply go around the room, have everyone introduce themselves, and ask for their input on the problem. (*Note:* It is the facilitator's responsibility to make sure that everyone stays in character.)

In the *excursion* technique, you intentionally bring the group to another place or time. For instance, in looking for innovative ideas for an interior design firm, I once had the group take an excursion to the Wild West. There, as we "saw" several horses drinking from the same water trough, we realized that a cooperative venture to produce and market a interior design video (to metaphorically share the water or resources) between our client and a fabric manufacturer made a great deal of marketing sense.

In another excursion when we were looking to generate names for a new cheese Frito line extension, we took an imaginary trip to a fishing boat in the South Pacific. We soon hooked the name "Great White Cheddar."

What if you or members of the group are having trouble imagining an exciting place to go? Create an excursion based on one of the fantasy jobs of your participants. It makes the session that much more personal—and therefore potentially exciting for your participants.

In the final technique related to the fantasy occupation exercise, the *wish* technique, you start by imagining that a magic genie has granted you several wishes for anything that you might ever want. The wishes can be totally absurd and/or impractical. They can violate fundamental laws of nature—and, indeed, often the best wishes do. By entertaining wishes without limitations, it is often quite easy then, in step 2, to figure out a way to make a fancifully impractical idea a reality.

A good example of the wish technique in action is a creative session that I did for the American Camping Association in which I had a particularly difficult camp owner. This owner had been in the business for over 10 years and kept saying how he just could not imagine creating a new camp activity that (1) was new, (2) was affordable, and (3) the kids would like. So, we tried the wish technique. The results were wonderful even by the skeptical camp owner's admission. Two wishes that I particularly liked were to have Michael Jordan run a basketball clinic and Madonna give a free concert. Probably not in the camp's budget, right? But as we got to talking about how to approximate these wishes, we discovered a wonderful new camp project: Why not have the kids themselves become their favorite star? They could make up costumes, give performances, and motivational speeches, or do whatever it was they imagined their star doing if he or she were to visit the camp. It was a case of "when you wish upon a star / makes no difference who you are / your dreams come true."

Time Traveling for the Ultimate Jump Start

See if you can complete this sentence. After you have finished all the warm-up exercises, the best place to start your ideation session is ____

_____.

Somewhat paradoxically, I have found that the best place to start an ideation session is "at the end." What does starting "at the end" mean? Most experienced trainers know that it is important to set objectives and goals for a meeting. Establishing meeting objectives helps us to make the meeting more focused, efficient, and ultimately productive. Having well-defined meeting objectives also makes it easier for the leader to redirect the course of the meeting when he or she feels that the group has gotten off track. Ideation sessions, despite their being (hopefully) wide-open free-for-alls, can also benefit from having clearly defined ideation goals objectives. But, frankly, "starting at the end" means even more than simply setting meeting objectives. If you think of establishing meeting objectives as something that you do for the group, think of "starting at the end" as something that you do for each individual in the group.

To start the "start at the end" (or time track visualization as I call it) exercise, I have everyone imagine that it is now the end of the day. "Imagine," I say, "that we have just spent all day brainstorming and the results were nothing short of miraculous—a tremendously exciting and successful session."

"What made you so excited about the work we just did and the ideas we just created?" I ask each of the group members.

Invariably one group member will begin by saying, "I'd like to see us create an idea...." I quickly jump in and correct their phrasing. "What I *liked* about the ideas we created today...." I want to make sure that they are getting into the visualize-the-future, look-back-on-the-day spirit of the exercise.

The results of this simple exercise never fail to amaze me. It somehow personalizes the whole objective-setting process. Corporate objectives are transformed into more immediate, heartfelt and important personal objectives. The ill-defined and often unattained goal of ownership has become a reality.

> "I like that we *created* a $100 million new-product idea that has the potential to revitalize this company."

> "I love that everyone *worked together* today to create several ideas that I know will save our department several million dollars."

> "I'm excited that we *created* a name for this new brand that the consumer will both love and remember."

In addition to generating ownership, this time track visualization exercise has some very important other benefits. For one, it helps build a solid and powerful group identity. Paradoxically, because each person has had a chance to be heard and express his or her desire, the group as a whole can more easily come together *as a group* to help each person to reach their specific ideational objective for the day. Everyone knows where everyone else wants to go and, as a rule, feels good about helping them to get there.

The importance of this group identity effect should not be underestimated. I recently facilitated a new service ideation session for a Malcolm Baldrige quality award winner. A dozen of the company's most creative and forward-thinking executives participated in the session. Unfortunately (as I found out later), many of the executives also disliked one another. Somewhat surprisingly, this was one of the most successful sessions, both from the standpoint of ideas created, and team spirit engendered, that I have ever conducted. Two of the executives came up to me after the session and said that it was this opening time track visualization exercise that was in large part responsible for setting such a positive tone (and ultimately successful result) for the day's activities.

A second very positive result of this exercise is that it helps the consultant, both consciously and subconsciously, to facilitate the session. It gives the consultant an accurate picture (not to mention feeling) of the needs, motives, and goals of each participant. Armed with this knowledge, the facilitator can more effectively direct the session down avenues of ideational thought that he or she intuitively feels have the greatest potential for success. It is difficult to know where you should be leading the group if you don't know where everyone *wants* to go.

Finally, the time track visualization exercise provides both the consultant and the client with an effective tool for determining how successful the session ultimately was. I am always a little surprised that somehow, almost magically, the group invariably manages to accomplish *all* its visualized results.

HOW TO IMPLEMENT CONTINUOUS QUALITY IMPROVEMENT IN A PROJECT MANAGEMENT ENVIRONMENT

Phil Ventresca and Tom Flynn

Phil Ventresca *is president of Advanced Management Services, Inc. (968 Washington St., Stoughton, MA 02072, 617-344-1103, 73662,3326@compuserve.com), a management development consultancy specializing in total quality. Phil is the program director for the Massachusetts chapter of the American Society for Training and Development and the vice-chairman of Programs for Project Management Institutes New Product Development Specific Interest Group.* **Tom Flynn** *is an AMS project consultant as well as president of T. A. Flynn & Associates. Phil and Tom are adjunct faculty members at Boston University Center for Management Development. They have co-authored* **High Performance Quality, People and Process: Tools for Continuous Improvement** *(Advanced Management Sources, 1955).*

"People and process together improve quality." So say the authors of this guide, as they illustrate how the concepts of High Performance Quality™ can best be applied to project teams and project management. This guide incorporates a simple representation of continuous improvement methodology, the making of a peanut butter and jelly sandwich, to illustrate how you can apply these quality management principles to your own project management environment.

High Performance Quality™ (HPQ) is a systematic approach to developing a corporate structure that will deliver continuous quality improvement (CQI). The principles of HPQ are based on the merger of two concepts: total quality management (TQM) and hazard analysis critical control point (HACCP), a process control system. It integrates the basic principles of systems thinking, individual and collective accountability, consensus decision making, continuous learning, and scientific quality methods.

When implemented under the umbrella of TQM concepts, HACCP becomes a powerful tool to enhance management accuracy and decision making. This process of hazard analysis and critical control point determination can be applied to all tasks within a process and project. It becomes a continuous circle throughout a project, addressing each individual task and creating a foundation for continuous improvement.

The HACCP concept has been used in the manufacturing industry for decades. It has been utilized by NASA and the federal government's Natick Labs. The Pillsbury Company brought the principles into the food industry. Pillsbury used the system to produce food for the U.S. Space Program to assure that it would not be contaminated with pathogens that could cause illness, resulting in a catastrophic mission.

Traditional quality control measures that rely on end product testing are reactive in nature. With the merging of TQM and HACCP concepts, a proactive approach can be established. By implementing the HPQ system, the ultimate customer can be assured of product quality, service, reliability, and, just as important, on-time and on-budget project completion.

By focusing on and modifying a process within a project for continuous improvement, the HPQ system provides a more specific and critical approach to managing than traditional inspection and quality control approaches. Forward-thinking quality practitioners understand that the change and downsizing associated with improvement efforts can represent negative effects for the people involved. A continuous improvement effort focused only on process will fail. Hence the HPQ approach: people and process together improve quality. If the project manager and the team cannot win, then the project is destined for disaster.

In today's changing business environment, programs, concepts, and people change. HPQ is an interchangeable system that contributes to any quality-based environment by building on existing technology. It is a mindset that can take hold in any existing project environment to initiate and continually improve results. The methodology is not a new twist on TQM or another fad. It is a proven, time-tested, quality-based system that focuses on process control and people development. It provides data for continuous process improvement, skills enhancement, and customer satisfaction.

Before you can implement the mechanics of the system, it is necessary to establish the principles of continuous improvement throughout your organization and project team. Develop the following principles to drive continuous improvement efforts:

✓ Identify the improvement opportunity.

✓ Develop customer-focused purpose.

✓ Formulate improvement objectives.

✓ Enlist a cross-functional improvement team.

✓ Plan, do, check, act.

✓ Implement improvement.

✓ Continuously learn and train.

The strategic steps of the process improvement effort are as follows:

✓ *Needs assessment and quality planning:* designing strategies and analyzing gaps

✓ *Control points:* identifying risks at customer contact points

✓ *Development of quality standards:* critical limits for policy and performance review

✓ *Control point monitoring procedures:* customer-focused process accuracy

✓ *Establish modifying actions:* critical path modifications for management process

✓ *Documentation:* record keeping

✓ *Procedures to verify program effectiveness:* process improvement

Quality concepts apply to all stages of a process and, when you come right down to it, all stages of your everyday life. Everyone uses these tools in some way everyday. Quality concepts developed through this type of system are easy-to-understand resource management techniques.

Manage *things,* lead *people.* It is all part of your job.

The constant stream of documented action against objectives will provide accurate data to utilize in team and customer reviews. Utilizing this system requires the interaction of both internal and external customer groups.

Figure 34.1 demonstrates how HPQ creates a circle of process control and utilizes the data to initiate proactive change, leading to customer satisfaction and continuous improvement. Applying these steps to all projects will provide control for each individual task and process that make up the network schedule and furnish data for future planning and improvement. This cycle of continuous improvement can be utilized at various points throughout a project and as a framework encompassing many projects. It simply represents a quality toolbox.

The Peanut Butter and Jelly Sandwich Process Improvement Task

Overview: In order to illustrate the concepts of continuous improvement, you have been assigned the following task. The task is a simplistic representation of continuous improvement methodology. The task is part of a larger project called making lunch. The finished task will meet the total lunch project at the end of the production day. Your team can work to improve another task within the PBJ process or select an example from your world. If you select an improvement opportunity from your work situation to practice using the system, be sure the team has enough knowledge to work together efficiently. Utilize the examples illustrated to model your efforts against.

Improvement objective: Your team is being asked to identify why peanut butter and jelly sandwiches are weighing out of specification (overweight) after the application of peanut butter. Weight checks

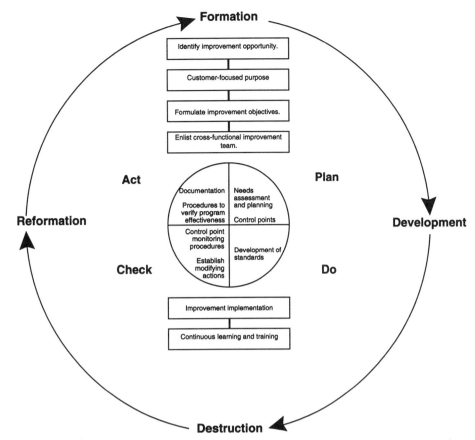

Figure 34.1.

conclude that the product meets specifications to the point of peanut butter application. Due to equipment restrictions, the weight check is performed after the peanut butter is applied to the bread.

Tools and methods selected for this example are meant to expose you to the basic procedures for continuous improvement. These procedures can be applied to any project, production process or service system that is not functioning efficiently.

Task description: Production of 100 peanut butter and jelly sandwiches per day

Specifications: White bread, two 1.0-oz slices per sandwich, ±0.01-oz variance per slice

Grape jelly, 1.0 oz per sandwich, ±0.03-oz variance

Smooth peanut butter, 1.0 oz per sandwich, ±0.20-oz variance

Cross cut

Total sandwich weight: 4.0 oz, ±0.25-oz variance

✓ White bread is purchased from a vendor who slices to exact weight specifications of a 1.0-oz slice. Weight is monitored at delivery in random lots as part of the vendor specifications program. No regular variance has been detected in the history of business with this vendor. Bread is set on an assembly line after opening packages.

✓ One ounce of jelly is applied to one piece of bread through a tube dispenser system. Each application is weighed electronically by computer and automatically ejected onto the bread. The machine is checked for calibration hourly and tuned daily. Bread with jelly continues down the production line.

✓ One ounce of peanut butter is applied manually with an ounce measurement spoon. It is scraped clean and leveled with a knife. Peanut butter is applied to the bread. Spreading is manual due to clogging in the automatic machine tubes. Spoons meet vendor specifications and are purchased from multiple suppliers. The second piece of bread is put on the sandwich manually using the same bread as the first process step (1.0 oz).

✓ The finished sandwich is weighed to ensure specification within acceptable variance levels. The customer has allowed for a total sandwich weight variation of 0.25 oz. To this point, the PBJ company has set standards for variance at each control point not to exceed the total product variance. Due to the existing situation and low system performance, the PBJ Company has allowed for 0.20 of the total variance coming from the PB. This has met with some customer dissatisfaction due to unsatisfactory mouth feel. The PBJ Company is relying on continuous improvement efforts to help tighten this spec so that they can maintain and grow their business. The customer has made it known that they are looking for a supplier who can run production on a tighter spec.

✓ Sandwiches are crosscut with a mechanical cutter before exiting the line.

✓ Sandwiches are cellophane wrapped and packed in a master case labeled and set for shipping.

Organize the project team assigned to this improvement task.

Organizing Quality-driven Teams

Teams outperform individuals, especially when performance requires multiple skills, judgments, and experiences. Remember, there is no "I" in team. The dynamics associated with teams can become unfocused if set guidelines are not implemented during meetings.

The first step to effectively utilize the team is to define the roles.

Meeting Roles

✓ *Team leader:* The leader manages the meeting process.

✓ *Recorder:* The recorder writes significant meeting content and decisions on a flip chart.

✓ *Facilitator:* The facilitator is an advisor or consultant to the team.

✓ *Team member:* All members participate actively.

Using groups or teams to improve quality gains several benefits for an organization:

✓ Team members deepen their understanding of their own work.

✓ Commitment and motivation are boosted.

✓ Better decisions can be made because the team has more complete knowledge about the process.

Utilize the following steps to ensure productive meetings:

✓ Clarify the meeting objectives.

✓ Review the roles.

✓ Review the agenda.

✓ Work through the agenda items.

✓ Review the meeting record.

✓ Plan next steps and the next meeting agenda.

✓ Evaluate the meeting.

As a team member, you are empowered to make creative contributions to the focused effort. Utilize consensus decision-making and idea-generating tools to help to improve the process. The following tips can help develop this process.

Consensus Decision-making Tools

Multiple Voting

✓ Agree on the criteria for selecting ideas.

✓ Identify each idea on the list with a letter of the alphabet.

✓ Agree on the number of ideas for which each member will vote.

✓ Vote individually on paper, listing the letter of each selected idea.

✓ Take turns calling out the letters of selected ideas.

✓ Record and add the votes on a flip chart.

✓ Decide which ideas should receive further consideration.

Rank Ordering

✓ Agree on the criteria for ranking ideas.

✓ Identify each idea on the list with a letter of the alphabet.

✓ Individually list the letters on paper and indicate the rank of each idea, with 1 being the first choice.

✓ Take turns calling out the ranking of ideas.

✓ Analyze the results, looking at both the total for each idea and the individual rankings.

Structured Discussion

✓ Agree on the criteria for the decision.

✓ Lead a group to consensus on a list of five or fewer ideas.

✓ Take turns expressing points of view without interactive discussion or debate.

✓ Summarize points of agreement after all members have had an opportunity to speak uninterrupted.

✓ Debate and discuss conflicting ideas.

✓ Periodically check for agreement by asking each member to state his or her point of view.

✓ Continue to discuss and debate the ideas until a decision is reached.

Idea-generating Tools

Brainstorming

✓ Clarify the brainstorming objective.

✓ Call out ideas in turn around the group.

✓ Record each idea on a flip chart.

✓ Build on and expand the ideas of others.

✓ Pass when an idea does not come quickly to mind.

✓ Resist stopping when ideas slow down.

✓ Clarify each idea and eliminate exact duplicates after all ideas are listed.

Nominal Group Technique

✓ Clarify the nominal group objective.

✓ Individually list as many ideas as possible.

✓ Call out ideas from the lists in turn around the group.

✓ Record each idea on a flip chart.

✓ Pass when all ideas on a list have been presented.

✓ Clarify each idea and eliminate exact duplicates when all ideas are listed.

It is imperative to listen to both the voice of the customer and the voice of the process during process evaluation, strategic planning, and data collection. Issues and conflict left unresolved from team meetings will not go away. Utilize team meetings to clarify and focus objectives and include customer and vendor representatives when possible.

If your customers and primary vendors are represented at team meetings, they share the buy-in. Management of a task is easier when you have an agreement on need with all parties responsible for completion.

Encourage entrepreneurial thinking. Corporate cloning is contradictory to improvement efforts and can stifle innovation. Manage a task as if it were your personal vision. The power of that enthusiasm will spread over your team and results-driven decision making will take shape.

Team leaders must avoid the reverse responsibility syndrome. No one has to be a hero. Hold the team members individually and collectively accountable.

The following agenda can be utilized as a guide for the PBJ team meeting:

AGENDA

PBJ Process Improvement Meeting Roles

Team leader

Recorder

Facilitator

Multilevel team members, production, front line, and so on

Customer representative

Vendor representatives

Meeting Objective: to identify causes leading to the effect of overweight PBJ sandwiches after the point of PB application

Team Discussion Topics

✓ Design an improvement opportunity statement
✓ Data collection and Pareto analysis
✓ Flow chart process
✓ Root cause analysis, fishbone diagram
✓ Utilize force field analysis
✓ Flow chart improved process
✓ Determine quality standards to measure against
✓ Measurements
✓ Corrective actions
✓ Process variation, control charts
✓ Plan, do, check, act for continuous improvement

Evaluate the meeting against objectives.

The team discussion topics are predetermined as a guide and based on HPQ system components.

Improvement Statement

An improvement statement represents the daily track over which you travel. Developing an improvement statement defines why we need to improve the task. In a way, it puts boundaries around the process. This is our understanding of what our client and our company have chartered us to accomplish.

On the journey of continuous improvement, the improvement statement tells us where we are going and what it is going to be like when we get there. If we were to classify this statement in general terms, it would encompass a vision and mission.

Utilize your team skills to formulate a comprehensive improvement statement. Your team will find comfort knowing that they have a set of agreed-upon rules and focused objectives. This will enhance the buy-in and commitment of each team member who participates in the development.

Data Collection and Pareto Analysis

The following is an outline of the Pareto analysis tool that can be used to illustrate priorities from data collection. The objective is to discover why PBJ sandwiches are overweight after the application of peanut butter to bread.

Utilize the description of the process previously outlined to better determine the priorities that should be more closely looked at. In a more complicated situation, a flow chart of the entire process should be reviewed in order to select start and end points for the improvement efforts.

A Pareto analysis is a descending bar graph used to illustrate and prioritize the most important processes to work on first or to demonstrate how different units of comparison affect the prioritization of categories. In our case, it identifies the most significant cause of a problem or effect so that we can prepare improvements to stabilize a process. The first and highest bar traditionally indicates the number one priority. The left side of the graph represents the unit of comparison. The right side illustrates percentages. A line should be drawn across the chart, graphing the cumulative percentages.

Once complete, look for evidence of the Pareto principle, traditionally known as the 80/20 rule. If 20% of your categories represent 80% of your responses, the Pareto principle is evident and you have identified an area that needs to be looked at closer.

Many forms of data collection are applicable at this point. In general, select one that will render a fair cross section of data. This data collection and prioritization format can be used for service, manufacturing, project, reengineering, and many other applications. Remember, define objectives and predetermine measurements before starting data collection or Pareto analysis. The data will be further analyzed by the team.

These data were provided to the team upon request. The team defined what areas could have the most amount of causes leading to the undesired effect. They prioritized based on several categories. The objective was to determine what causes could be having the most influence on the effect (the overweight PB sandwiches after PB application). By selecting and stratifying the data collected, our team can initiate a closer investigation of the causes. This first step in data collection is imperative to create efficiency during problem solving. The team chose weight variation as the measurement due to the identified problem, and they chose to stratify the data based on the known process steps that were closest to the affected area.

The Pareto analysis in Figure 34.2 seeks to verify if the weight variation is coming from one or more of the speculated components in the PBJ manufacturing process by plotting the number of variances from standard at each given weight measurement point. The figure clearly shows that 80% of the per week variances were identified after the peanut butter had been applied. The other two categories, bread weight and jelly application, accounted for a very small percentage of variance. By looking at these results, it is clear that the team needs to further analyze the process from the point of PB application, including that step. Utilize a flow chart to visualize the existing process.

Flow Chart Process

If you are to manage, change, or improve a process, the flow chart will help to visualize the critical elements. If you cannot see it, you cannot

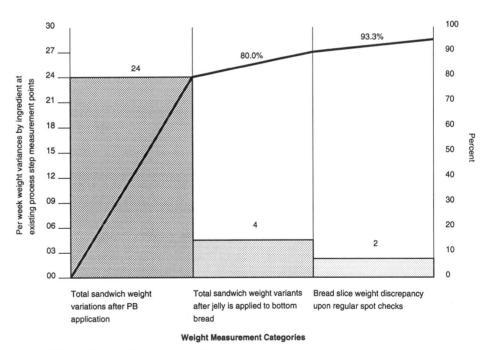

Figure 34.2. Weight Measurement Categories.

be proactive to it. A flow chart can be used to look closer at an individual task within the project. The flow chart can help project managers find more efficient methods within an individual task that could improve efficiency throughout the project. Apply the flow chart to the process or task identified as a priority during data collection.

Considered one of the simplest tools, the flow chart can be as basic or technically intricate as the process it is used to illustrate. The flow chart is used to provide a visual representation of any process. Each type of process step is traditionally identified on the chart by a standardized geometric shape. A flow chart illustrates a process from start to finish and should include every step in between.

Take all variables into consideration and concentrate on the agreed-upon objectives.

Follow these steps to assist in the exercise.

✓ Determine the frame or boundaries of the process.

✓ Determine the steps in the process.

✓ Sequence the steps.

The flow chart in Figure 34.3 represents a snapshot of the overall process determined as having the most likelihood of causing the identified effect. It is being utilized as a microscope to analyze in minute detail the portion of this process that the team has identified for improvement.

Utilize the team through brainstorming to identify causes contributing to the effect based on the existing flow chart of the process.

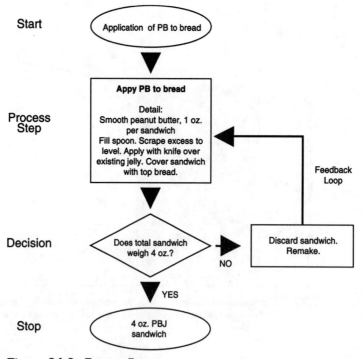

Figure 34.3. Existing Process.

Consensus decision making can be used by the team again in this exercise to further refine the speculated causes.

The fishbone diagram in Figure 34.5 can be used to look closer at specific related causes and effects.

Root Cause Analysis: Fishbone Diagram

Figure 34.4 helps to visualize the importance of root cause identification. The fishbone diagram is also known as the cause and effect diagram. It is primarily used to track down the root cause of a known problem (effect). It methodically provides the answer to the general question of what could be causing this problem. Once the general cause is identified, begin asking why. By continuously investigating the why for each cause, the root cause may be more concisely identified.

Applying a fishbone analysis at the point at which one discovers a problem or a process that needs improvement will save time in the long run. The true root cause of a problem is not always the obvious option. If you only react to symptoms of a problem, you will need to continually modify your process. Resolution of the root cause, once identified, could provide a permanent fix for a series of problems.

The traditional construction of the fishbone diagram involves identifying the effect, or symptom, on the right side of the diagram. The primary cause categories are identified through group brainstorming.

For example, *PBJ sandwich weighs out of spec after application of PB.* You recognized this problem by monitoring during the process. Remember, in total-quality-based projects, you measure the process, not the end product. This equals "quality built in." As a project manager, it is your responsibility to find and resolve the root cause so that the process can be made more efficient. This will help you to reduce slippage from time line and budgets by being proactive to possible risks.

Identify the four major factors affecting your particular process problem. For the purpose of this exercise, we are using method, per-

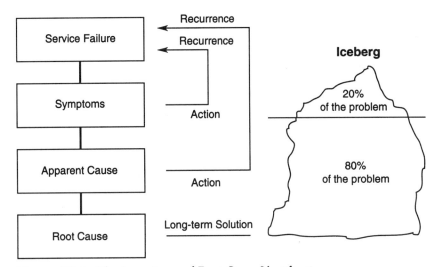

Figure 34.4. The Importance of Root Cause Identification.

sonnel, materials, and machinery (see Figure 34.5). These can be adapted to your specific situation. More bones can be added to specifically identify a particular process.

By utilizing the data from the fishbone, the team came to consensus decision that measuring spoons and manual application of peanut butter are the sources of the problem. They outlined a solution by suggesting a review of the spec on the equipment with the supplier. As a secondary note, they decided to weigh the PB before application by changing the process steps. The team performed a cost analysis to determine that it is more costly to remake sandwiches than it is to make modifications to the procedure.

By utilizing this chart, they identified the common steps that could affect the total sandwich weight. From this discussion, the team generated ideas to improve the process.

Use the team to analyze the improvement ideas. Establish critical control points and prepare the boundaries to formulate the new improved process flow chart.

As part of the modifications, the team needed to develop a control system that would provide better data reporting and would allow for immediate proactive action against any future out-of-control process variance.

They began work to identify critical control points that could be applied to the process modification proposal. The team will finalize a complete proposal for corporate approval of needed changes before making process changes. The customer can also be included in these approval meetings.

When you have identified the control points, adjust the flow chart to show the improved process; then implement the standards for your controls. This method of process control will help to deliver zero-defect results as the process is brought back to life.

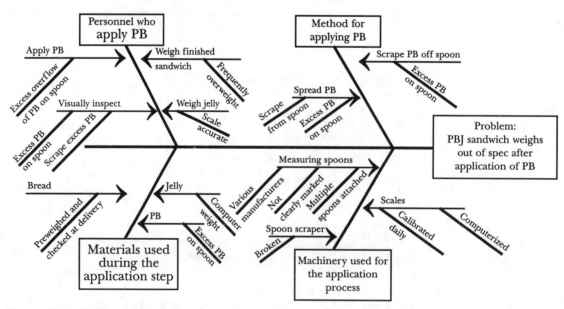

Figure 34.5. Fishbone Diagram.

The team works together at this point to rechart the process and make improvements. Decisions are made along the way. The team utilized the following tool to help clarify the decisions and identify critical steps.

Force Field Analysis

Deciding on a critical control point within a team environment can lead to disagreement. To assist in your decision-making process, utilize a force field analysis. You should also incorporate group decision-making tools in this process. A force field analysis identifies the forces and factors in place that support or work against the solution of an issue or problem so that the positives can be reinforced and the negatives eliminated or reduced. When implemented, it will

✓ Present the positives and negatives of a situation.

✓ Force people to think together.

✓ Encourage people to agree about the relative priority of factors on each side of the balance sheet.

✓ Encourage reflection on the underlying roots of a problem and its solution.

Designing a Force Field Analysis

If a critical control point (CCP) cannot be clearly identified by the team during the brainstorming session associated with flow charting, use this sample assessment technique to develop further consensus about the classification of a control point. A *critical control point* is a step or procedure where a risk to process success can be prevented, eliminated, or reduced. For example, try to identify process steps as critical control points. That is, is the application of peanut butter to bread a critical control point?

If the team disagrees on the classification of control points, apply the analysis. List positive and negative thoughts regarding the question. By utilizing these tools together with the flow chart, your decision will become clearer.

Is the application of peanut butter to bread a critical control point?

Driving Forces: *Why Critical*	*Restraining Forces:* *Why Not Critical*
Remaking sandwiches is adding cost and time.	Not weighing peanut butter before the application will speed the process.
Too much peanut butter will alter the finished weight of the sandwich.	Weighing on bread will require less equipment cleaning time.
Weighing after application will result in discarding of the entire sandwich.	
Too much peanut butter will increase the cost of ingredients.	

The decision is clear. The application step is a critical control point. The driving forces far outweigh the restraining forces.

The following tools can help you to set standards to measure the accuracy of your process. This renders accountability against agreement on need and standards.

The objective is to eliminate waste from the system by identifying where it can occur and productively monitor that point in the process. Flow chart the improved process and incorporate the critical control points, as in Figure 34.6.

The team redefined the process by moving a weight measurement back to the most likely place where the process was failing. They took an educated approach to this change based on the data prioritization.

A cost analysis was performed to conclude that the purchase of a scale and the added worker-hour time to operate it would be far less expensive than the cost of rework required due to overweight sandwiches. The team was able to tighten the spec on the PB application, adding value to the process for the customer. They were also able to create new specifications based on the customer's request to tighten specs.

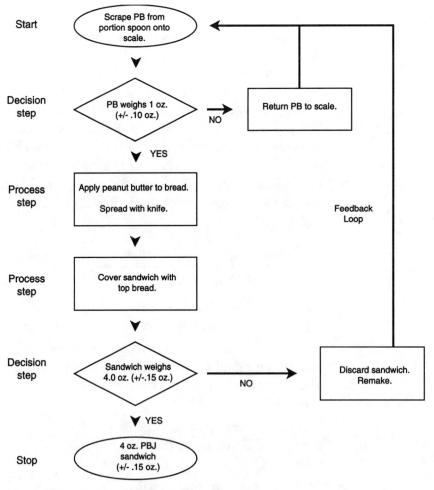

Figure 34.6. Improved Process Flow Chart.

White bread, two 1.0-oz slices per sandwich, ±0.01-oz variance per slice

Grape jelly, 1.0 oz per sandwich, ±0.03-oz variance

Smooth peanut butter, 1.0 oz per sandwich, ±0.10-oz variance

Cross cut

Total sandwich weight: 4.0 oz ±0.15-oz variance

The following tools will help to customize policy and procedure around the improvement.

Determine Quality Standards to Measure Against

When assigning quality standards, your goal is zero defects. Quality is either there or it is not. Use the team to set measurable standards against customer objectives and process requirements.

Utilize this step to identify each process critical control point and the acceptable standard to be met at the CCP. To define standards, include team negotiation, results, and vendor–customer interaction.

Critical Control Point	Standard
Apply 1 oz of peanut butter to each sandwich	1.0-oz peanut butter +0.10 to −0.10 acceptable variance

A standard can also be referred to as a critical limit. If a process varies outside the critical limit, it is said to be out of control and corrective action is initiated.

Measurements

Depending on your specific environment or process, different measurement tools can be used. For our process step of applying peanut butter, a weight measurement is utilized.

CCP	Standard	Measurement
Apply peanut butter to bread	1.0 oz of peanut butter +0.10 to −0.10 acceptable variance	Weigh on calibrated scale before application to bread Acceptable range at 1.0 ± 0.10 oz must be met

In reality, variance will always occur. Process improvement needs to take place when it is out of control due to special causes. Our ability to predict risk can reduce problems. However, it is still necessary to plan corrective actions.

A corrective action is put in place for failure against a standard within a process. Taking corrective action at predetermined control points will reduce the risk of total process failure. Remember, measure throughout the process. Corrective action should be taken when out-of-control variance is detected at a measurement step.

Critical Control Point	Standard	Measurement	Corrective Action
Application of PB to bread	1.0 oz of peanut butter, +0.10 to –0.10 acceptable variance	Weigh on calibrated scale scale before the application to bread. Acceptable range of 1.0 oz ± 0.10 oz	Retrain workers to check ounce marking on spoon. Confirm spoon volume by checking output weight on calibrated scale. Reinforce spec with spoon supplier.

Return out-of-weight spec PB to source and continue process.

All data compiled from process monitoring should be recorded for future use and tracking. This standardized form can become part of a standard operations procedure manual if the process is going to recur.

The control chart in Figure 34.7 will record variance for reference and allow you to formulate a history. In the case of a defined start and end project, this form of checks and balances during a project life cycle can be applied against milestones. Note that a critical control point does not have to be a milestone. In all likelihood, you will have more critical control points than milestones.

Process Variation, Control Charts

Since variation is a natural part of any process, it is inappropriate and wasteful to modify a process every time it results in a measurably different product. On the other hand, it is fiscal suicide to allow a process to develop excessive levels of variation. The solution, of course, is to monitor all processes and modify them only when there is too much change. This philosophy should also be applied to the level of success at milestones.

A control chart (Figure 34.7) will enable you to track variation in a process, task, or project in real time. The upper and lower controls are calculated after a series of sample products from a process have been taken or specific negotiation regarding the requirements has been completed. If a process evaluation is to be of any real value, it must be completed honestly and objectively. Adjusting a process even slightly during the data–gathering phase may make your process look better, but such adjustments can make truly effective change much more difficult to institute.

You are asked to produce 100 PBJ sandwiches. If a variance is not recognized during early stages of production, the process will fail.

Control charts can be maintained for all measurable critical control points in a process, as well as for total project performance against time line and budget. This form of record keeping will allow project managers to review process accuracy and adjust in real time.

Utilize the control chart to record variation of PB sandwich weight before and after the modifying action to provide support for successful modifications. The team will now compile all data for recommendations for permanent process improvements. Implementation can now take place and continued improvement should occur.

By utilizing real-time measurement, we were able to recognize the variance in time to correct the process. Measure the process. End product testing would have rendered a dissatisfied customer and financial loss or project failure.

Plan, Do, Check, and Act for Continuous Improvement

The concept of review is a basic step in continuous improvement. All processes are reviewed on a regular basis, utilizing the plan, do, check, and act, or PICA, format (see Figure 34.8).

All processes are under continual evaluation and therefore constant improvement. Standardizing allows an organization the opportunity to incorporate an improvement from one area into the process of all similar areas. Improved quality processes are too valuable to use on a limited basis.

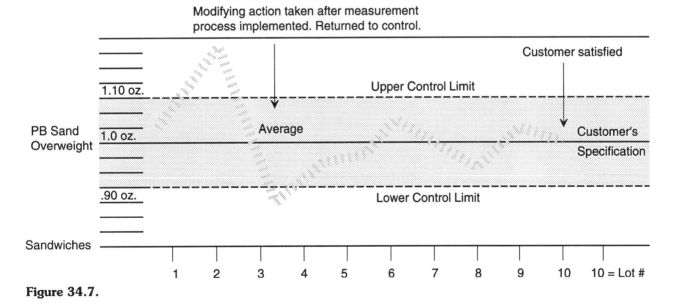

Figure 34.7.

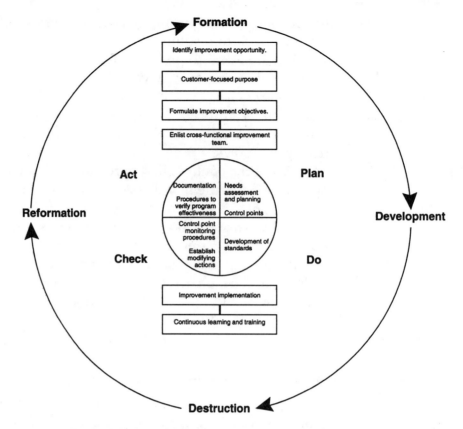

Figure 34.8. HPQ: A Model for Continuous Improvement.

Data and documentation on people and processes from the PBJ task can help to plan other similar tasks. Project managers overseeing several projects with similar elements can share data as part of cross-functional teaming.

All changes developed through the HPQ process are carefully tied to the satisfaction of the customer. The effort to improve process and quality is never-ending. Providing goods and services that delight the ultimate customer is the number one objective. These results are attainable by anyone initiating a mindset of excellence.

Psychology of Change: Keeping People in the Process

As a project manager in a changing environment, you must adapt to a new business environment. Managers are being called on to manage situations, not just processes. A project manager moving into the 21st century will have the tools and skills to manage client expectations, customer satisfaction, and people within the process. Future thinking concepts are designed to spark thought processes away from the system and put them on the people. You have heard the voice of the process. This is the voice of the customer.

Every defect is a treasure. Managing effectively in an environment of change requires a willingness to reinterpret the everyday methods of operation. *Kaizen* is a fundamental Japanese societal concept that views change as a constant flux of opportunities. Kaizen combines the possibilities to improve quality, productivity, and effectiveness in personal and professional life.

Kaizen is a word that means small improvements. Management supports kaizen by means of suggestion programs or by allowing time for teams to meet. If management sets a tone of receptivity to new ideas, it will foster innovation through empowerment. Standard teams become high-powered project teams.

Management must be secure enough to realize that chipping away at the paradigm is the only way to remain competitive. When the continuous improvement initiative is implemented throughout projects, customer satisfaction results.

HOW TO DEVELOP
ORGANIZATIONAL VISION

Richard Allen

Richard K. Allen, *Ph.D., has been a professor of interpersonal communication at Central Michigan University for 28 years. His interest and teaching areas are organizational communication, training and development, communication and change, and persuasion. Dick is also a consultant in these same areas and he can be reached at 911 Glen Ave., Mt. Pleasant, MI 48858, 517-772-3109.*

An organization without an agreed-upon, clearly articulated vision is like a ship without a rudder, an airplane without a flight plan. You need only to look around at recently successful organizations that are now in serious trouble to realize that, without a clear vision and a plan to articulate that vision, any organization and/or individual will surely perish.

This visioning action guide is intended to encompass all organizational stakeholders. The model fosters participative agreement concerning where your organization is now and a vision for what you want to be (desired end result) as well as the means by which you intend to reach that end result. Use this model for setting a vision for your work group, division, department, or entire organization.

A corporate-level vision enables organizations to have direction, to efficiently plan for the future, and to be able to work together to accomplish goals. However, it has become very clear, and at the same time surprising, that many of the most successful corporations do not have a clear corporate vision. Consultants say that when they bring the key people in a corporation together there is often great surprise among these key people themselves at how little agreement they have concerning the corporate vision. If the organization has no clear, agreed-upon vision, it is difficult for them to know if they are heading in the right direction at any given time.

The need for a clear vision is important at all levels from entire organizations to each individual in these organizations. It should also be obvious that it is equally important to have an agreement between your personal vision for your own future and the vision of your organization. However, this agreement is hard to achieve if these visions are not clearly articulated.

This visioning model, or action plan, is divided into four stages. The first two stages ask for an individual, independent perception of the current organizational vision from all organizational members. The third stage requires the management team to come to consensus on the organizational vision and set goals and measurable objectives. The final stage asks each manager to sit down with his or her associates (team members) and together set vision-based individual goals and measurable objectives. The following provides an overview of these four stages.

Stage 1: In the first stage, the management team responds to a visioning instrument. The organizational levels to be included in this stage are optional. The instrument should include questions concerning the current state of visioning in the organization, how clear the organizational vision is, and, most important, a request for each respondent to write down his or her version of the current organizational vision. There are off-the-shelf instruments that will work just fine here, but many organizations may want to create their own specific instruments. It is very important that everyone filling out this form do so independently and, at the same time, without consulting one another and without prior notice. The results will be more effective if the responses are spontaneous and individualized.

Stage 2: Closely following this first stage, all organizational members will be asked to respond individually and independently. These other organizational members will fill out an instrument similar to the one used in stage 1. However, it might be appropriate to scale down this instrument to accommodate the knowledge level of the recipients.

Stage 3: Once these visioning forms have been completed, the management team will meet to compare its perceptions of the corporate vision with those of their managerial colleagues, as well as with the organizational vision statements of their associates.

During these management planning meetings, normally a surprising amount of shock and disbelief is revealed concerning the amount of discrepancy and differences of opinion between the participants regarding the organizational vision. During this management meeting stage it is helpful to address such questions as who, where, and what the organization is now and who, where, and what it wants to be. The goal of this meeting should be to reach total consensus right there on the spot concerning an agreed-upon organizational vision that can be written down and articulated. Once consensus has been reached concerning the organizational vision, the group must articulate a set of general goals, an action plan to bring the vision to fruition as well as the specific measurable objectives necessary to carry out the goals. Remember that a vision (end) is not the same as an action plan (means). A vision without an action plan is just a dream; an action plan without a vision is drudgery; a vision and an action plan are your best hope for the future.

This action plan consisting of goal- and objective-setting activities may be done at the visioning meeting or at a subsequent meeting or meetings to be called as soon as possible. The goals and objectives should always be kept within the parameters of the agreed-upon vision. The goal- and objective-setting task can be handled by the management team or in consultation with other or all organizational associates, depending on the commitment to participation currently existing in the organization.

Stage 4: After the vision, goals, and objectives have been set, your organization can move into the final stage of the model. In this final stage, each manager and supervisor at each level will take the opportunity to sit down with each team member to participatively and jointly agree on an individual vision for each team member. Of course, the individual vision needs to be within the parameters of the agreed-upon organizational vision, as well as being specific to the individual's position and functional responsibilities within your organization. The managers and their team members can then proceed to set measurable, agreed-upon individual goals and objectives. These individual goals and objectives may possibly even alter job descriptions.

Summary

The ideal outcome expected from the application of this model is an organization that knows who it is, what it wants to be, and how to get there. An even greater expectation is an organization that, if it went back to the first two steps in the model, would independently write down an identical organizational vision; everyone in the organization would be running in the same direction. And remember that no matter how well the model and the visioning process itself works, it means nothing unless every organizational member is unified concerning the vision and puts the vision into practice on a daily basis.

REFERENCES

Bennis, W. 1992, November. *Leadership for the 90s.* Presented as part of the Wayne State University "Leaders on Leadership" series, Detroit, MI.

Info-Line. July 1991. *How to Develop a Vision* (Issue 107). Alexandria, VA: American Society for Training and Development.

Lee, C. 1993. The vision thing. *Training,* February, 25–34.

Morrisey, G. L. 1992. Your personal mission statement: A foundation for the future. *Training & Development,* November, 71–74.

Naisbitt, J. 1984. *Megatrends: Ten New Directions Transforming Your Lives* (2nd ed). New York: Warner Books.

Peters, T. J., and R. H. Waterman, Jr. 1982. *In Search of Excellence.* New York: Harper & Row.

HOW TO TRANSFORM AN ORGANIZATION THROUGH CRITERION-REFERENCED TESTING

William Coscarelli and Sharon Shrock

Bill Coscarelli *is a professor of instructional technology at Southern Illinois University (Department of Curriculum and Instruction, Carbondale, IL 62901), 618-453-4218, 71502.3501@compuserv.com) and past president of the National Society for Performance and Instruction.* **Sharon Shrock** *is an associate professor and coordinator of the instructional development and instructional technology graduate specializations within the department of curriculum and instruction at Southern Illinois University (618-453-4217). Both are regular consultants to global organizations in the areas of evaluation and assessment systems. Their book* **Criterion-referenced Test Development: Technical and Legal Guidelines for Corporate Trainers** *(Addison-Wesley, 1989) has won two national professional society awards as the outstanding book of the year.*

Organizational development professionals typically see themselves as active creators of change in organizations. However, significant and important change interventions can come from unanticipated parts of the organization. This guide is designed to help organizational developers to understand the consequences of valid criterion-referenced tests within an organization and to consider managing such change as potentially transformational to the organization.

Change management professionals tend to think of their role as proactively analyzing, designing, developing, implementing, and evaluating organizational structures. Yet managers are responding to competitive forces that create organizations in a nearly continual state of flux, and these managers often create changes that can have far reaching effects for an organization—but only to the extent that such changes can be absorbed. Because organizations are systemic beings, the change management professional needs to actively scan for such interventions because they can come from unexpected quarters. The case studies here offer the change management professional two perspectives: (1) profound implications for change can come from seemingly distant parts of an organization, and (2) with increased management interest in accountability, the type of testing systems (criterion-referenced) described in these two case studies may become a trend in organizations within the next decade.

In most large organizations, testing systems usually reside in one of two places: personnel or training. Additionally, these two departments often reflect the different philosophies of test use: criterion referenced versus norm-referenced. Essentially, norm-referenced tests are composed of items that will separate the scores of test takers from one another. A norm-referenced test (NRT) interpretation defines the performance of test takers in relation to one another. Norm-referenced tests are constructed using a statistically based method. This means that items are chosen for inclusion on the test that have been shown to reliably separate test takers; the SATs and the Medical College Admission Test are examples of NRTs. Personnel departments often use such tests to select people for a job or predict future success in an assignment.

In contrast to NRTs, the criterion-referenced test (CRT) defines the performance of each test taker without regard to the performance of others. A CRT is based on items that assess a specific competency. Most corporate training philosophies specify such an objectives-based system. Unlike the NRT, by which success is defined in terms of being ahead of someone else, the CRT interpretation defines success as being able to perform a specific task or set of competencies; for example, was the landing gear positioned properly?

Why Are Reliable and Valid CRTs Important?

Criterion-referenced tests are important for several reasons. First, there is an ethical obligation to treat people in an honest and fair manner—something a well-designed CRT will do regardless of race, creed, or color. Second, it is our professional duty to provide accurate assessments of our instructional interventions (or individual competence when no instruction is present, for example, a "test-out" or equivalency exam). The reliable and valid CRT will not allow us to ignore failures in the training process, which will likely have consequences for performance on the job as well as affect management's return on investment in training.

While there are a number of purposes for using a CRT in training, we want to concentrate on those tests that represent the "calipers" of the instructional process: posttests (administered after instruction to assess the test taker's mastery of terminal objectives, that is, end-of-course objectives) and equivalency tests (used to determine whether a learner has already mastered the course's terminal objectives without going through instruction).

Imagine that you are positioned at the end of a steel mill production line. Holding a pair of calipers that may have cost only $10, you are responsible for determining whether or not a finished piece of steel meets the standard of thickness set for the production run. With your $10 tool, you may find yourself in the position of stopping the entire production process if you find sheet metal that does not meet the standard. Asking why the steel does not meet specifications could unleash a wide range of possibilities (a thickness setting was off, machinery needs to be replaced, employees are unmotivated or untrained to produce the product, and so on), all because of the accuracy of a single measurement device. Such is the nature of criterion-referenced tests (CRTs), and such are the consequences of serious implementation of the CRT process in an organization.

Once an organization takes CRT testing seriously by creating reliable and valid tests (that can no more be impugned for their accuracy than the accuracy of reliable and valid calipers), employee success or failure in the training and testing process will not be ignored by management. Consequently, CRT implementation will no longer be thought of as simply a box in the instructional development model, but rather the likely beginning of an organizational transformation.

Problems with the Role of Organizational Development in Corporate CRT

Let's assume for the moment that for ethical, professional, and economic interests we wish to create valid CRTs. How would we go about doing so given the status quo—with its range of forces that inhibit such change? Well, there is good news and bad news. First, the good news. Organizational development (OD) is a systematic technology for taking an organization as it is and making it more effective in what it does. OD answers the following question, as Fletcher (1990, p. 84) notes: "How can I make the organization more effective?" OD is a technology for planned organizational change that has a rich history to guide us.

OD as a change process usually begins by identifying several roles: Who is the change sponsor responsible for legitimizing the change? Who is the change agent responsible for implementing the change? Who is the target audience that is expected to adopt the change? Who are the resisters? the opinion leaders? the decision makers?

With these roles in mind, the OD specialist then begins a process of guiding the innovation, in our case criterion-referenced testing systems, through a series of stages. Dormant and Smith (1986) summarized these stages as awareness, interest, evaluation, trial, and integration. For each of these stages the change agent operates in different roles to facilitate Lewin's notion of "unfreezing and refreezing." During *awareness,* the agent acts as an *advertiser* to provide information. During *interest,* the agent is a *counselor* who understands adopter concerns and provides cognitive and emotional support. When the adopter moves to *evaluation,* the agent serves as a *demonstrator* who pilots or facilitates the piloting of the innovation within the organization. In the *trial* stage, the adopter seeks to implement the innovation, and the agent now serves as an *instructor* and colleague who provides the necessary skills for implementing the innovation. Finally, as the innovation is *integrated* into the organization, the agent becomes a *technical assistant* who provides the necessary technical support and cultural observation to help nurture and sustain the innovation.

Thus if we view criterion-referenced testing as an OD issue and not just instructional technology, then we should expect to integrate CRT technology by adopting a change paradigm. That's the good news. Now, the bad news. Organizational development won't work—its the wrong paradigm!

Why Is OD the Wrong Paradigm?

OD will not work for two reasons:

✓ OD works best for small groups with relatively similar goals whose purpose for change is to develop new behaviors that will operate within the current goal structure, not large organizations with internally competing interests; but, more importantly,

✓ OD techniques don't work for a transformational, systemic change, which is what criterion-referenced testing is. Implementing criterion-referenced testing, for ethical, professional, or economic reasons, will constitute a paradigm shift for our corporations because CRTs will introduce a unique level of personal and organizational accountability that will not easily be ignored or glossed over.

The appropriate paradigm for integrating criterion-referenced testing is organizational transformation.

What Is Organizational Transformation and Why Does It Apply to CRTs?

Organizational transformation (OT) is a relatively new vision of the change process in organizations. Fletcher (1990) provides an informative review of the alternative definitions of transformational change and notes Kilman and Covin's argument (Fletcher, p. 11) that the idea of organizational transformation warrants inclusion in change and management theory—that it is more than new jargon for an old idea.

✓ Transformational changes are those that provide a profound, fundamental change of "perceptions, values, and consciousness" in the organization. Such change is really revolutionary, rather than evolutionary, and results in the organization seeing itself in a radically new manner.

✓ OT is a systemic, holistic response to demands from the environment. It answers the question "How can I visualize this organization so that it serves the world in a new way?" (Fletcher, 1990, p. 84). Johnston (1987) feels that OT is the creation of a new, discontinuous context, while OD involves refinement and strengthening of behaviors in a current repertoire. In other words, we see OT as a paradigmatic shift within the organization whose significance parallels Kuhn's notion of paradigm shift in his book *The Structure of Scientific Revolutions* (1970).

OT can be differentiated from:

✓ *Minor changes,* those that involve a modification of behaviors and attitudes without affecting the system's core, and

✓ *Major changes,* those that cause an organization to develop a new perspective and act in new ways, but without a fundamental shift in the system's core.

We have worked with two international corporations who have attempted to place CRT systems within their current structure. In one, they viewed the CRT process as part of their ongoing instructional development process. They felt that by establishing valid tests they could make defensible decisions (for economic, ethical, and professional reasons) on new employee skills. Their CRT system disintegrated totally when it became apparent that those identified as nonmasters were failing not because of their own lack of diligence, but due to managerial indifference and response to other organizational contingencies. The managers were threatened and the system was soon emasculated—in one evening, when a very powerful regional vice-president announced "We have no failures here, only winners." What was once a strong CRT system now became a sophisticated coaching system for new hires. The failure for this organization was to view CRT as part of the instructional technology process, that is, the last box in an ID model and therefore as only "minor change."

In another international company, the CRT process was begun when a senior vice-president raised the issue of accountability for the company's training division:

✓ What did the participants really learn as a result of training?

✓ What did they take back to the job?

✓ What was the return-on-investment from training?

A task force was convened and determined that a CRT system was the professional and ethical response to the use of testing for any decision that might affect an individual's promotion or merit. In addition, by emphasizing learner mastery in training and fair testing, the company could begin to develop accurate responses to these three types of questions. However, it was not long before a number of constituents within the organization began to undermine the process. Employees realized that they would now be in a situation where test results could be used to justify layoffs; the legal department felt that no testing was better than any testing, because any testing would inevitably lead to lawsuits that would be costly and time consuming; personnel felt much the same as legal, plus they brought a testing philosophy that was based on norm-referenced tests for personnel selection and were therefore uncomfortable with the CRT process; managers found that there was no reward for removing employees from time on the job, for example, sales calls, when they were being expected to make unit sales quotas; instructional designers resisted because they were not given training, time, and resources to execute the new demands. Despite the use of many traditional OD techniques (task forces, pilot projects, and the like), failure came because CRT was viewed only as "major change."

CRT as Organizational Transformation

A comprehensive CRT system will have a radical effect on current values, attitudes, and behaviors because it is a professional, ethical, and economic means to establish accountability and feedback within the organization. Well-designed CRT systems allow for scores to be reported and used as part of the organization's internal assessment process in measuring its progress toward organizational goals—the vision. Because CRT will significantly affect internal systems and external system interactions, for example, the grievance and legal systems, it must be viewed as organizational transformation in order to survive. CRT means that adults will take tests that are fair, and they therefore demand instruction that is competent, based on skills that are needed. Managers will have to be rewarded to support goals associated with testing, and internal personnel and legal systems will have to be reconstrued to develop an understanding of testing based on standards of mastery, not of comparison. And all these changes occur in spite of the fact that adults don't like tests and, even worse, nearly every test reminds them of being a child, not an adult.

Organizational transformation begins with a top-down approach to change. OT depends on its leaders, who appear to share certain qualities:

✓ They have a vision of what the future of the organization will be. Their vision is shared and supported, mystically, through rituals, symbols, and stories that reinforce and illustrate the vision.

✓ They mobilize commitment on the part of those who will help them to sponsor the vision. These sustaining sponsors will use their resources to navigate toward the vision.

✓ They institutionalize the changes needed through new or modified patterns of communication, problem solving, or decision making.

✓ They seek to attract or develop employees with a sense of empowerment.

Empowerment, in fact, appears to be a critical foundation toward OT. Empowerment is the individual belief that a person can influence his or her own destiny.

Empowered people do not think they control all elements of their life, but they do believe that most of the time they are responsible for a great deal of what happens to them ... the antithesis of empowerment is "victimization," in which people feel that they are trapped with no options.... Victims resent being used and tend to feel defeated. They therefore demonstrate little interest in contributing beyond what is necessary to protect their employment.... Empowered employees and managers appreciate being fully utilized and feel enriched by their work experience. (OD Resources, 1991, p. 6)

Tichy and Ulrich (1984, p. 165) also add that a transformed organization is one in which decisions and structures are developed with an understanding of equity, justice, power, and freedom.

A transformed organization is built on a foundation of empowerment, which enables the organization to function with participative management techniques. These techniques are necessary because of the synergistic work environments required to react to the increasingly rapid changes needed for an organization to meet is business objectives. (OD Resources, 1991, p. 2)

Change Principles That Will Be Transforming

Generally, five principles for transformational change will apply to CRTs (and other technologies):

1. Intervention begins at the top of the management structure, never at the bottom, the "grass roots."

2. Significant change will not happen without a continuous and visible commitment by a sponsor at the highest functional level.

3. A sponsor must establish a cascade structure of support in which a subordinate manager at each lower level will sustain the change. Strong sustaining sponsors will ensure accurate and durable change. Weak sponsors must be educated or replaced, otherwise failure is inevitable (OD Resources, 1989, p. 14).

4. The initiating sponsor's vision must be communicated in such a way that the cost of maintaining the status quo is more painful than making the change. (Most people are frightened of a transition state that may be ego or economically threatening and will therefore seek to avoid the new state except under often painful situations.) The sponsor must present a vision and manage the contingencies so that the status quo is seen as painful (for either the organization or the individual) because it represents either a loss of dominance or a missed opportunity.

5. Initiating and sustaining sponsors must make structural and organizational rewards within the organization that are compatible with the change.

What Does Establishing CRTs in an Organization Mean to the Change Specialist?

The general procedures for establishing CRTs follow logically from the principles that we have just discussed:

1. Management at the highest possible level within the organization must support the implementation of CRTs and make it apparent to all that it is a priority. If it does not, CRTs will remain only as a box in the ID model—useful for improving the training function, but not transformational for the organization.

2. People must be expected to use the test results for decisions, such that the results of the tests are seen to have immediate and strategic payoff: immediate payoff in terms of personal promotion or merit and strategic payoff in that mastery of skills and knowledge is seen as contributing to the search for organizational excellence.

3. Coordination with the various personnel constituencies is imperative, for example, legal and personnel. Support services for the technical aspects of testing, for example, optical scanning systems, computer-based testing, and reporting forms, must be created and maintained.

4. Managers must be rewarded monetarily, professionally, and/or symbolically for their assistance in executing and maintaining the transformation.

Conclusion

Creating change in an organization is always a daunting process. With the reality of global competition settling in on organizations, the need to adapt, and adapt quickly, has become standard operating procedure for successful companies. Traditional models for organizational development may have once emphasized the nature of a systematic approach to analysis, design, and implementation of an innovation; but the pace of change may create unanticipated consequences that need to be identified and managed in a timely manner. We have tried to show that (1) as a specific tool, criterion-referenced testing technology is becoming a part of management's vocabulary; (2) CRTs are only an example of a larger challenge—change that can begin in one part of the organization and have serious consequences for all of the organization; (3) scanning to identify and integrate these types of change should become an active part of the change management process; and (4) the OD paradigm may prove inadequate for systemic changes that are more transformational than developmental to an organization.

REFERENCES

Dormant, D., in M. Smith (ed.). 1986. *Human Performance Technology: An Introduction.* Bloomington, IN: National Society for Performance and Technology.

Fletcher, B. R. 1990. *Organizational Transformation Theorists and Practitioners.* New York: Praeger Publishers.

Johnston, R. W. January 1987. Integrating organizational development with spirituality. *Journal of Religion and the Applied Behavioral Sciences,* pp. 5–9.

Kuhn, T. S. 1970. *The Structure of Scientific Revolutions.* Chicago: University of Chicago Press.

Levy, A., and U. Merry. 1986. *Organizational Transformation: Approaches, Strategies, Theories.* New York: Praeger Publishers.

Odiorne, G. S. 1981. *The Change Resisters.* Upper Saddle River, NJ: Prentice Hall.

OD Resources. 1989. *Gaining acceptance for performance technology in your organization.* Paper presented at the annual meeting of the National Society for Performance and Technology, Toronto, Ontario.

OD Resources. 1991. *Key findings regarding "empowerment" and "participative management" during change.* Atlanta, GA.

Shrock, S. A., and W. C. Coscarelli. 1989. *Criterion-referenced Test Development: Technical and Legal Guidelines for Corporate Training.* Reading, MA: Addison-Wesley Publishing Co.

Tichy, N. M. 1983. *Managing Strategic Change: Technical, Political, and Cultural Dynamics.* New York: John Wiley & Sons.

Tichy, N. M., D. O. Ulrich. 1984. In G. Morgan (ed.). *Creative Organization Theory: A Resourcebook.* Newbury Park, CA: Sage Publications, pp. 163–165.

HOW TO DEVELOP A HEALTHY WORK ENVIRONMENT

R. Scott Olds and Patrick O'Connor

R. Scott Olds, *HS.D., is an associate professor of health education at Kent State University (316 White Hall, Kent, OH 44242, 216-672-7977, rolds@kentvm.kent.edu). He teaches both undergraduate and graduate professional preparation courses in health education. Dr. Olds's research interests are in systems-level community change and information technology that help promote public health.* **Patrick J. O'Connor,** *Ed.D, is currently an associate professor in the College of Education at Kent State University (300 White Hall, Kent, OH 44242, 216-672-2656, poconnor@kentvm.kent.edu). He teaches graduate courses in training, organizational development, leadership, and teacher preparation. His research interests are in organizational change and workforce development. He is the author of* **Personal Selling** *(Macmillan, 1990) and* **Retailing** *(Delmar, 1981).*

Promoting a healthy work environment is cost-effective and helps save lives and improve employee health and productivity. This guide describes four steps to take to introduce and implement a healthy work environment plan of action.

Health care insurance premiums are rising at the staggering rate of 16% annually. Many companies attempt to reduce their premium burden by forcing workers to pay higher copayments and deductibles. Although these practices have helped to slightly lower the rate of increase, such cost shifting has provided management with short-term relief at best, while increasing financial demands on an already strained American workforce. To help ease some of that tension, companies have begun touting health promotion programs to improve employee health and reduce health care costs. Corporations are finding that many insurance carriers will negotiate smaller increases if a company can draw a clear correlation between on-site health promotion programs and fewer health insurance claims. For example, Standard Telephone Company saved $27,290 on their 1992 annual health policy premium (3% discount) through such negotiation with the Traveler's Insurance Company. Steelcase, Inc., in Grand Rapids, Michigan, reduced health care costs by $618 per identified high-risk employee over a three-year time period. The cost-effectiveness and benefit from participating in work site health promotion programs are well established and becoming an increasingly important factor in cost control planning.

Although typically perceived from a physical perspective, health also includes social and emotional components that together affect the general health of the American workforce. The leading causes of death (heart disease, cancer, and injury) can be prevented if certain health strategies are employed. When left unchecked, the exorbitant costs associated with these problems will continue to escalate and create a serious threat to our economic competitiveness and profitability. Current estimates project health care costs are approaching $5000 per person in the United States by the year 2000! Prevention offers three distinct advantages: (1) It saves money, (2) it saves lives, and (3) it improves the quality of life.

As much as 30% of all employer-paid health care costs are due to acquired, unhealthy life-style habits. Former GM Chair Roger Smith said that "if well-designed health promotion programs at work help people stay healthier, then employees and employers will pay lower insurance premiums, and health care costs will be better contained." The Worksite Health Promotion Alliance recommends that these unhealthy habits can be changed through health promotion and disease prevention programs. Such programs can substantially reduce the number of sick days, outpatient costs, and hospitalization costs for participating businesses. However, employers and employees need to consider a new paradigm for viewing health in the workplace in order for these outcomes to be realized. The approach will require employers to establish a systems perspective. In effect, the entire culture of the organization must be addressed. Everything from employee orientation to performance incentives should be directed toward the goal of creating and maintaining a healthy work environment.

Controlling health care costs and improving employee health to increase productivity and worker satisfaction can be addressed through a systems approach to developing a healthy work environment. An essential element of this approach embraces a culture grounded in prevention, not treatment. A good example of this approach is being carried out at the 3M tape manufacturing company in Cynthiana, Kentucky. Management at 3M has begun to shift emphasis to preventive efforts. Their commitment to this initiative is best illustrated by their willingness to offer employees health promotion programs on company time. Another good illustration is the health promotion program set up at Tenneco in 1981. Over the last 14 years since Tenneco's program was started, the percentage of smokers has decreased from 32% to 10%, and 40% of their employees now regularly exercise compared with 25% at the program's beginning. Tenneco's program has increased productivity and employee retention and reduced absenteeism, worker injury, and medical and workers' compensation costs.

The system approach closely parallels the total quality management efforts common in many workplaces today. Both approaches consider behavior change, prevention, a customer focus, statistical process control and attention to outcomes. The national office of the American Cancer Society further illustrates the application of TQM in their reorganization and commitment to cancer control. Thus, the purpose of this guide is to offer practical steps for developing a healthy work environment using a systems approach.

Four Steps toward a Healthy Work Environment

An organization can move toward a productive, healthy work environment by employing the following four-step process. Procedures within each step should be closely followed to achieve a systems approach to reaching the goal of a healthy work environment that can improve employee health, which leads to a happier, more productive, and less costly employee. The bottom line in business can only be improved through such efforts.

Step I: Conduct a Health Audit

A health audit enables the human resource personnel to determine a health profile of the employees and the entire organization. This is essential to developing a comprehensive action plan for creating the healthy work environment. Identifying goals, developing intervention strategies, and monitoring progress are much easier after completing the health audit. The health audit consists of three interrelated activities.

1. A survey of employee's health beliefs and behaviors helps to identify employee perceptions of the importance of health in their personal and work lives. This survey can be completed using a questionnaire, employee interviews, or even focus groups. This type of information and the process used to collect it help to create the healthy culture that is necessary for effective health promotion program development.

2. Gather secondary data to determine the status of health-related factors within the organization. Such data include insurance claims, accident reports, absenteeism, and chronic illnesses (heart disease, stroke, cancer) and help to identify trends or patterns related to the health status of the organization. These trends can be further analyzed to determine how, where, and what company health promotion priorities should be established.

3. Review and integrate current health promotion activities within the organization. Most organizations are involved with various health-related intervention programs, although larger companies (50 or more employees) are more likely to offer such programs, and the areas of programming most common are stress management and fitness strategies. However, frequently, these activities are unconnected. It is important to view all intervention strategies as part of a larger, systems approach to creating a healthy work environment.

Step II: Establish a Cross-functional Team

It is most common for senior management to be responsible for carrying out health promotion activities at the work site. In addition, we argue that a cross-functional team should be established to coordinate the efforts of human resource personnel. This diversely represented team is charged with creating an action plan that establishes and maintains a healthy work environment. The team should focus on the following three activities.

1. Identify selection criteria for setting priorities related to the action plan. Urgency, type, and frequency of insurance claims and cost and number of employees affected are sample criteria that the team could consider. These selection criteria will be unique to each organization.

2. The team should review the secondary data gathered in step I and establish priorities based on the preceding selection criteria. This effort may also include identifying specific employee populations where a critical need exists or the greatest cost savings can be realized.

3. The team should now incorporate the priorities into the action plan. The plan should identify personnel, resources, and the time line for implementing intervention strategies. The plan should also identify methods for monitoring progress. Collecting additional data regarding the selection criteria (accidents, insurance claims, and the like) is a standard way to determine the progress of the plan.

Step III: Implement the Action Plan

The human resource area in the organization should coordinate the implementation of the action plan. The cross-functional work team should assist and advise where necessary. To ensure that a systems approach is employed, the following areas should be considered in developing the action plan:

1. A clear set of objectives for the health promotion program needs to be decided based on the health audit completed in step I. The objectives should be specific, time exact, measurable, and prioritized. Doing so will increase the likelihood of attaining these objectives while also providing a clear opportunity to monitor and measure such attainment.

2. Personnel from the cross-functional teams need to establish subcommittee structures for planning, implementing (interventions), and monitoring the program.

3. Policy decisions should be made regarding the intervention strategies designed to foster a healthy work environment. For example, policies regarding safety in materials handling should be estab-

lished, expressed, and followed. Furthermore, flexible work hours, where appropriate, should be encouraged to allow time to engage in the designated intervention. Most successful companies provide employees with time during the workday to engage in such activity. As mentioned earlier, 3M provides a good illustration of the type of culture considered necessary to successfully implement health promotion strategies.

4. Training can be considered an intervention approach. Training in safety procedures, for example, should be part of an employee orientation program. This should ultimately reduce the number of injuries on the job. This support is necessary to sustain the intervention so that the health promotion practice becomes a part of the culture of the workplace.

5. An incentive system for employee recognition and reward should be considered. Employees typically respond to positive recognition, and this principle can be applied to promote a healthy work environment. For example, reaching a specific goal related to production time lost due to accidents may result in a reward to individual or groups of employees. In addition to the provision of increased salary as an obvious incentive, employees favorably respond to praise and appreciation for the contribution that they make to their work setting.

6. Physical adjustments where needed may contribute to a healthy work environment. For example, a ventilation system may reduce the amount of toxic fumes in a work setting. Or asbestos removal may contribute to improved air quality in the workplace. Providing employees access to fitness facilities either on site or close by is helpful to encourage employees to make physical activity a regular part of their schedule.

7. Family members should be included in the action plan. Employees are directly affected by those with whom they live and socialize. Thus, these individuals should be active and voluntary participants in the health promotion intervention. This will help to strengthen the probability of successful adoption of healthy behaviors that affect both home and work.

Step IV: Monitor Progress

Monitoring the implementation and outcome of the action plan is essential. The following suggestions are offered:

1. Be sure that the action plan has a well-conceived monitoring plan established prior to implementation.

2. Frequently seek feedback from participants through direct and indirect means. The cross-functional team should have regular access to this information so that, if modifications in the intervention are necessary, they can be made during rather than after the program.

3. Identify specific sources and methods of obtaining data that will help to determine how well the intervention reached the specific objectives.

4. Establish a communication(s) channel that will let employees know about programs and the progress of them.

Points to Remember When Developing a Healthy
Work Environment

Promoting a healthy work environment is cost-effective and helps to save lives and improve employee health. Points to remember include the following:

✓ Select one program, do it well, and build from that success.

✓ Communicate efforts freely and frequently so that everyone is aware of the action plan.

✓ Provide organizational structure and support, including staff, budget, strategic planning, and symbolic leadership.

✓ Emphasize prevention, education, and health promotion in the organizational culture, rather than as a punitive posture.

✓ Participation in any program should be voluntary. Constantly monitor intervention approaches and strategies to determine progress and necessary modifications.

HOW TO MANAGE PERSONAL CONFLICTS AMONG TEAM MEMBERS

Donna Robbins

Donna Robbins, *Ph.D., is an organization development consultant who specializes in the issues facing companies that must change the way that they do business. She can be reached at 1513 Escondida Court, Santa Fe, New Mexico 87506, 505-438-2553. Donna's postdoctoral studies at the Gestalt Therapy Institute and her clinical experience enable her to work effectively with resistance to change. Donna is also an adjunct professor at Pepperdine University, Graduate School of Education and Psychology.*

You have been brought in as a consultant to assist a team that seemingly has everything going for it: intelligent members, supportive management, and a definite mission. Yet something is definitely wrong. The team is completely unproductive during its meetings, and the tension is so thick among the team members that you can even feel your stomach tighten when you are with the group. What is going on here? The following guide details two accounts of team dynamics gone wrong. In both cases, underlying personal conflicts among the team members prevented the group from making even the most basic progress at work. Read how you can work to manage these conflicts and dramatically improve the overall performance of a team.

Team 1: The Case of the Elusive Employee

You have been asked to consult with a group of 13 team members, including the manager, Ed. The employees have averaged three years on the job. Prior to meeting with the group as a whole, you conduct individual interviews in which you ask the members to discuss their feelings and experiences about their work group and the organization at large. The individual interviews reveal the following:

✓ Ed believes that all 13 employees are well trained and highly competent.

✓ Most of the group members respect each other and seek each other's opinions on projects.

✓ Most jobs are completed individually, but when large projects come up, nearly everyone pitches in.

✓ No one tries to get all the glory or "one-up" anyone else.

✓ Ed is both respected for his technical skills and well liked by the staff.

Your Problem

During the individual interviews, everyone except Ed mentions a problem with one of their colleagues—Tom. According to all reports, Tom arrives at work around 10:00 A.M., takes a 2-hour lunch, and leaves for the day at about 3:00 P.M. The group members claim that Tom has been doing this since he was first hired, which was nearly a year ago. Furthermore, the group reports that Tom has isolated himself, refusing offers of lunch or other contact with his colleagues. Tom's colleagues resent his absences. They gossip about him and tell "Tom jokes," but no one ever confronts him directly. Several individuals have reported Tom's behavior to Ed, who has promised to take action.

During his individual interview, Ed never mentions Tom's disappearances until you bring it up. Ed appears embarrassed and says he had initiated disciplinary procedures after several employees had complained about Tom. Ed admits that he has dropped the ball by not following up on the disciplinary action. He seems surprised to learn that it was "such a big deal" to the group members. You are surprised that it is not a big deal to Ed! Interestingly, the group members are not angry with Ed, but instead focus all their resentment on Tom.

According to the team members, things came to a head one Friday afternoon when the group called an unscheduled meeting to discuss a problem concerning a major client. Tom had information that was crucial to a solution, but he was nowhere to be found. No one else had the information, and the client could not wait, so two group members volunteered to stay and resolve the situation. It took the volunteers all Friday night and most of Saturday to solve the problem. On Monday, several group members confronted Tom and expressed their anger. Tom refused to talk with them and walked away.

Your Resolution

Your challenge is to uncover the reasons for Tom's irresponsible work habits as well as for Ed's apparent disregard for Tom's effect on others. After synthesizing the data from the individual interviews, you arrange a joint meeting with Tom and Ed. When you describe the group's resentment of his disappearances, Tom responds that this is a private matter between Ed and himself. He expresses anger at you for "meddling," and at his team members for "gossiping behind his back." When you say that you believe they *had* come to him after the recent problem with his client, Tom becomes enraged, saying, "This has nothing to do with them! I fixed that problem when I got in on Monday!" When you point out that Tom's colleagues had worked Friday night and most of Saturday because he was not there to help, Tom leaves the room, slamming the door behind him.

Ed tells you he wants a chance to pick up the "dropped ball." He requests another meeting with Tom and asks you to be present. Ed schedules the meeting late in the week to give Tom a chance to cool off and do some thinking. In this meeting, Ed tells Tom that disappearing from work was negatively affecting the customers as well as the whole group and could not continue. Tom is not overtly angry, although he still insists his behavior is a private matter between himself and Ed.

Your next step is to arrange a two-day team-building session to discuss issues that are preventing the group from working together. When Tom hears about the session, he asks you if the Friday/Saturday incident will be mentioned. You tell him that if someone brings it up, it will be openly discussed.

During the team building, five people do tell Tom how his disappearances negatively affected their work. Tom seems unmoved and makes no response, but neither does he seem angry. An hour before the end of the team building session, Tom asks to speak. He acknowledges his lack of consideration and promises not to "pull his disappearing act again." He tells the group that he has always felt like an outsider. Since no one ever asks for his opinions or help, he assumes that the team has no respect for him. Someone asks if that is why he has kept his distance. Tom says it is. The colleague responds that he has had no sense of Tom's competence because they have had almost no contact with each other.

Another group member responds similarly. She goes on to say that she resents his disappearances so much that she purposely stays away from him. A few others express the same sentiment. After the team building session ends, several of the guys ask Tom to join them for a game of basketball. Tom accepts. The next morning, you notice Tom having breakfast with several group members.

Although Tom's willingness to interact socially does not last long, his work behavior changes significantly. He now arrives to work on time, works cooperatively with his colleagues, takes reasonable lunch breaks, and stays until the end of the work day. The team's overall productivity level increases substantially as a result of Tom's improved contributions to the group.

Your Analysis

You could argue that this was a disciplinary issue that could have been handled by Ed or by Human Resource. Certainly, Ed should have taken corrective action when he first learned of the problem. But he didn't, and once the group became resentful of Tom's disappearances and began spending time being angry and gossiping, they lost energy that could have been used productively. When Tom's behavior affected the performance of the group, two lessons became evident: first, since personal conflicts were negatively affecting performance, only by dealing with them could normal business resume. Second, Tom's disappearances became a team issue, and not simply an issue between Ed and himself. Even if Tom had stopped disappearing, the team would still have unresolved resentment.

The strategy used here was to directly and openly address the personal conflicts first in individual interviews, then in a joint session with the two most directly involved parties, and finally within a whole-group team-building session. This three-step approach allowed the team to vent their frustration and resentment, ultimately achieving the goal of putting the team back on track.

Team 2: The Case of the Miserable Manager

In a second situation, you have been asked to consult with a group that has very different personal dynamics. This team is made up of fifteen members: seven in system support, four in administration, three phone operators, and the manager. All of them use computers for data entry and word processing. Due to poor performance, upper management has asked you to hold a focus group with this team to determine what is and is not working. Once again you decide to begin your consulting work by conducting interviews with the team members. During the individual interviews, you learn the following:

✓ The three subgroups have rarely had an opportunity to work together. They remain separate both functionally and socially.

✓ Curt is the group's fifth manager in five years and is disliked by every member of the team.

✓ Everyone but Curt reports resentments and unresolved issues between group members. Curt denies any knowledge of such issues.

Your Problem

Your guess is that the manager, Curt, holds the key to understanding why this team is not working well together. You research Curt's employment history and come up with the following data: Curt has been with the company for nearly 30 years. Management sees him as a hard worker and a loyal employee. In the first of many recent company reorganizations, he was promoted to a first-line supervisory position where he supervised a group of three clerks. While his performance was unremarkable, the group did its job. Many first-line supervisory positions were eliminated during a second reorganization. At that time, Curt was two years from retirement. Rather than return him to employee status, he was kept in management. For a year, Curt worked on a special project and had no direct reports. His performance was adequate. When this new work group needed a new manager, Curt was put into the slot.

Your next step is to reanalyze the individual interviews for further hints as to how Curt's performance as a manager is affecting overall team productivity. The interviews with Curt's group revealed multiple problems that affect the group's functioning; however, none seems as serious as the team's negative feelings toward Curt. A cross-reference of the interviews show you that everyone has told you a similar story. About a year ago, when Curt first became manager, he told the team members that they would be required to rotate shifts, sometimes working days and sometimes nights. Previously, the night shift was covered by an individual who enjoyed working these hours. No one understood the need for the change and, when they protested, Curt gave no explanation other than to say, "That's the way it's going to be." One of the technicians, a single parent, was unable to arrange overnight care for her child. Curt told her that she would be demoted if she did not take her turn on the night shift. One of the other group members offered to work nights for her, but Curt would not allow this. The technician felt she had no choice and took the demotion.

The change of shifts incident demoralized the whole group. Since rotating shifts made no sense, the group assumed that Curt was vindictive. Several of them filed complaints with Human Resource and were told that the investigation would take some time. About five months after its inception, the rotating shifts were abruptly discontinued. No explanation was given, but the group members believed that their complaints to HR had been instrumental in reversing the policy. Eliminating the rotating shifts has reduced the level of group dissatisfaction, but it has done nothing to improve the relationship between Curt and his team.

More recently, Curt began a cross-training program. He told the group that this would increase productivity. The system support staff was expected to rotate on the phones and do some of the administrative work. The administrative and telephone staffs would learn to provide technical support to system users. The group members were required to train each other on an informal basis in their spare time. The group sees this as yet another indication of Curt's vindictiveness. Curt instituted the cross-training two months ago, but the heavy volume of work prohibited group members from training each other and implementing the policy. Still, it has hung over their heads, increasing the level of tension and the group's sense of helplessness.

During his individual interview, Curt gives brief responses to your questions, offering no details. He speaks of his job and his group in a flat tone of voice and makes almost no eye contact with you. When you mention the resentment the team felt about the rotating shifts, Curt shrugs. When you press for a response, he says, "That's how it was." When you ask why he instituted cross-training, Curt says, "That's how to get self-managed teams." By the end of the interview, you feel like you have been speaking to a machine rather than a thinking, feeling individual.

Your Resolution

The difficulty with this team seems to rest solely with the manager. Personal conflicts with the manager of this group are blocking whatever progress the rest of the team tries to make. After completing individual interviews and analyzing Curt's work history, you decide that it is now time to hold a whole-group discussion. Your goal for this team-building session is to try to get the personal conflicts between Curt and the other members of the group out into the open.

During the team-building session, all but two team members express feelings of hurt and helplessness about the rotating shifts and cross-training. The feedback to Curt is clear and direct. As in his individual interview, Curt makes almost no eye contact with anyone in the room. You try to prompt him to make verbal responses, yet even then he says little. Finally, Janet, a system support technician, speaks up.

Janet is about 30 years old and diminutive in stature and presence. Up to this point in the team building, she has said very little. Janet begins her feedback to Curt by asking him if he recalled the time she phoned him to say she was not at work because she had suffered a stroke, was partially paralyzed and in the hospital. Curt makes no response. She asks if he recalled his response to her. Curt shakes his head no. Janet continues, her voice starting to crack: "I was so scared, I didn't know what was happening to me. I guess I just wanted you to tell me not to worry about work and to concentrate on getting well. Instead, you asked me how many sick days I had left. You told me you would have to check the company policy to see how long I could stay in the hospital without losing pay." At this point Janet begins sobbing, as do several other group members. Curt still does not say a word. His body is rigid and he looks as though he is in a trance. He is, however, making eye contact with Janet. You move to Curt's side, and quietly say, "Curt, you have to say something to Janet. Can you think of something to say to her?" Curt nods yes, and after a long pause offers a shaky, "I didn't know." After another long pause, he adds, "I am sorry."

In that moment, it becomes obvious to everyone in the room that Curt is handicapped; he is unable to deal with even the most basic human emotions. Everyone witnesses the man that they had resented and feared become paralyzed when asked to make a simple, empathic response to his employee. In team follow-up sessions, many group members report that this was the moment that they stopped being afraid of Curt.

Your Analysis

In the year they spent under his management, everyone in the group held the same belief about Curt. They thought that he was vindictive and enjoyed bullying them. They thought that he enjoyed watching their helplessness. It was not until the team-building session that the group began to change their beliefs about him. In a sense, Curt's facade of vindictiveness dropped away to reveal him as both emotionally and intellectually handicapped. This new awareness is essential to the growth of the group since, when seen as vindictive, Curt was feared, but when seen as handicapped, Curt is pitied. When the group members gave up their fear of Curt, they also gave up their helplessness and are now able to develop new, more effective strategies for dealing with him. For example, several group members later report that they are now turning to each other for the support and direction that Curt cannot provide. One group member tells how he is now spending time with Curt, helping him interpret directives from his management and develop policy for the group. Almost everyone expresses resentment at having to support a manager who should be supporting them. However, others see it as a necessary nuisance until Curt is replaced.

Business was unproductive for the 14 members of Curt's group due to the personal conflicts between the team and its manager. Feelings interfered with the productivity of every individual in the group and business stalled. It is only after you give the group the opportunity to amplify and examine their personal grievances through individual interviews, team-building sessions, and follow-up discussions that the personal conflicts can recede into the background and the team can get on with its business.

HOW TO INTRODUCE CORPORATE CULTURE INTO YOUR HIRING PROCESS

Craig Toedtman

Craig B. Toedtman *is president of Resource Development Company, Inc. (402 Wood Drive, Suite 101, Blue Bell, PA 19422, 215-628-2293, XDBC45A@ Prodigy.com). The firm is a human resource management consulting firm specializing in building high-performance, quality-driven organizations. Craig is a certified senior professional in human resource and has been appointed by the Department of Commerce to the 1994 and 1995 Board of Examiners of the Malcolm Baldrige National Quality Award.*

The objective of any hiring process is to hire the right person ... at the right time ... for the right job. Too often there is a gap in this simple formula that causes the entire process to go awry. The gap is caused by the fact that candidates are not aware of the basic culture of a particular organization and only find out after they have been hired into a position that the organization's culture does not fit their own. Learn how to avoid unnecessary turnover by giving your potential new employees a real sense of the culture of your organization through the 15-step process detailed in this guide.

The culture of a work group is an invisible force that influences behavior. Culture is the unwritten, often invisible, influence that fills the void between policy and what actually takes place. Policies dictate, but culture formally decrees what really takes place through the interpretation of what policies say and what they leave out. As a result, potential employees need to experience the actual culture of the company that they are considering joining—before actually beginning employment.

It is a well-established fact that the best way to get to know a culture is to experience it. And that is exactly what you want to do with candidates for employment with your company. Give your candidates the opportunity to experience your company's culture firsthand. Let them come in and spend a day, or whatever amount of time is necessary, to get to know the environment *before* the start of employment.

You can supplement your hiring process with a day-long experience designed to give the hiring manager *and* the candidate firsthand knowledge of the candidate's fit into the new culture. People vary in many ways, some subtle and some not so subtle. Every person is unique. Combining the subtleties of individuals throughout an organization creates a culture that is also unique. These differences combine to present a source of strength as well as creativity for the organization.

The Hiring Process

You can incorporate a consideration of your organization's culture into the process of hiring a new employee in many different ways. Construct your approach to meet the objective of finding the qualified person who will add to, not detract from, the company's strengths. Here are 15 ways for you to introduce corporate culture into your hiring process.

1. *Review the content of the position and the skills required to be successful.* For example, describe the content of the position in general terms. The idea is to understand the basic function of the position to provide a good understanding of what is required to accomplish the purpose of the position. While some people like to have position descriptions as complete as possible with every task described in detail, there is a commonly accepted view that a system that describes the general features of the job, allowing freedom for creativity and accomplishment, is more often than not preferred.

2. *Include an analysis of the organization's culture on the position description.* For example, cultural analysis should include a discussion of the type of work environment. Is it nonbureaucratic; fast-paced; team-oriented; informal; high-pressure; high-walled; open; family-type atmosphere? What are the distinguishing characteristics of the environment? Is there a commitment to the customer or to quality? What management style exists, including is it people-oriented with a high level of independence? Are employees empowered? Are decisions top-down?

   What are the traits of the high performers, such as loyalty, dependability, initiative taking, self-imposed sense of urgency, business sense, organizational skills? Consider defining the high performer in terms of what is *not* descriptive, such as slow, not aggressive, poor listener, no follow-through, not a team player.

3. *Consider the background companies of qualifying applicants in terms of the culture that the applicant would be leaving.* For example, where has the applicant been working? Your company is a successful, top-down, autocratic organization with limited team-oriented problem-solving experience. The applicant has three years of experience at a team-oriented, consensus-driven organization, where people are empowered to make decisions. While this difference may not disqualify the applicant, it should cause you to probe and be con-

vinced that the differences will not result in a frustrated employee who likely will not remain long with the company.

Researching the applicant's background and the companies, departments, or work groups where she or he previously worked is a very important aspect in determining potential fit with your company, department, or work group. Spend time to understand the environment that the applicant is leaving and how it compares to your environment.

4. *Provide a good understanding of the type of place your company really is in initial interviews.* For example, a manufacturing engineer is being considered for a position with your company. Initial screening has resulted in your interest in bringing the candidate in for an initial interview. Your objective is to qualify the applicant prior to involving other members of the organization in the hiring process.

   The introductory interview should be held in the atmosphere that best represents the company. The applicant should get a sense of the pace, the organization, the interaction, and the demands of the position. The visit should include an in-depth tour of the company and in particular the work space of the applicant, answering the question "Does the applicant *really* fit in this environment?"

5. *Involve the candidate in a "day on the job" as part of the qualification process.* For example, assume that you are the engineering manager at a local manufacturer of consumer products and are in need of an additional engineer. You met the candidate at his initial interview, during which time you took him on an in-depth tour of the facility, and you have invited him back for a "day on the job." The day will begin with the hiring manager, 15 minutes or so, during which time the agenda for the day will be discussed.

6. *Provide an opportunity to meet and converse with the peers with whom the candidate will ultimately work.* For example, allocate an hour to be spent with two (or so) employees from the engineering department with whom the candidate would be working closely. They will give the candidate the opportunity to discuss the projects currently in process, the work environment, and any questions she or he might have about the department.

7. *Expose the candidate to the company's problem-solving style.* For example, a company with team-oriented problem solving should spend the next 1½ hours in a problem-solving exercise. The candidate can meet with a five- to six-member cross-functional team with which the candidate will be participating in a survival exercise. The team is comprised of employees with whom the candidate will come into contact during the normal course of successfully performing the job, including the cost accountant, shop foreman, and customer service representative. The exercise assumes that the team members were all victims of a plane crash. The objective is to prioritize the remaining items, ranking them from the most important to the

least important for use in surviving. Consensus is required within a certain time period. The candidate will experience working with potential peers in a problem-solving mode under the pressure of having to complete the assignment within a certain period of time.

8. *Give the candidate the opportunity to meet your cross-functional peers.* For example, during the next hour, the engineering candidate can meet with the product marketing manager (a peer of the hiring manager), who will review the current products and discuss the current market needs and the resulting impact on you as an engineer. Following lunch with the hiring manager, the candidate will meet with the company president, who will discuss the current vision, mission, and strategy in general, as well as how he or she sees the candidate fitting into them.

9. *Provide an in-depth look into the workings of your department.* For example, the last hour can be spent with you, the hiring manager. This is an opportunity to discuss the workings of the department, including hours and expectations. It is an opportunity to share your ideas and/or concerns about the position, the department, and/or the company. It is also an opportunity for the candidate to ask questions and share ideas and/or concerns.

   The candidate was included in the company culture for the day, experiencing problem-solving, meetings with peer groups, and having discussions with top management. It was an opportunity for the candidate to actually work with the people with whom he or she will ultimately work. There was value to the company and to the candidate: the company saw the candidate working within the culture, and the candidate experienced the culture first hand.

10. *Bring two (or several) candidates into the "day on the job" at the same time for added dimension.* For example, you are the manufacturing manager for a machine tool builder and have narrowed your candidates to two qualified individuals. Both candidates have experienced one-on-one interviews with you and several key members of management. All agree that the candidates meet the requirements of the position. Using the same agenda, both candidates are brought into the company for the day.

   There are several advantages to subjecting the candidates to the process simultaneously. The company has the advantage of seeing both finalists at the same time, and not having to think about the separate interviews to compare the applicants. The candidates have the benefit of hearing answers to questions that they would not have thought to ask. It is a win–win process, although it does put a lot of pressure on the candidates to meet their competition head on. For the right situation, this can be an enhancement to the hiring process.

   The process also exposes the candidates to employees from all areas. This enhances the candidates' understanding of the organization, at the same time increasing the chances for success on the job. The company representatives are *involved* in the hiring process and, by being so involved, they will do all that they can to assure the success for the candidate.

11. *Debrief the candidate(s) to further define company culture.* For example, "After spending time with representatives of the company, what thoughts do you have with regard to the position? the department? the company?" "What concerns do you have with regard to the position? the department? the company?" The hiring manager is showing concern for a potential employee—even before the first day of work!

12. *Ask questions that will provide an opportunity to explore how the candidate will fit in your company culture.* For example, following the interview process, the hiring manager provides an opportunity for the candidate to ask any questions that were not answered in the interview cycle. It is also an opportunity to weave in questions that will help to further describe the culture of the company. "Describe how you will apply imagination, ingenuity, and creativity to your job." The candidate who is able to do so would most likely not fit in a position that restricted imagination, ingenuity, and creativity.

    Ask for "an example of how you have worked independently with authorization from your manager to complete a task without his or her personal involvement." A person with the ability to act independently with the authority to complete a task would most likely have a tough adjustment to a culture with an autocratic, top-down management style of organizational behavior.

13. *Debrief the company representatives involved in the hiring process.* For example, the hiring manager should solicit feedback regarding the candidate(s) from company representatives involved in the hiring process. Having them involved is a total waste unless you hear what they have to say about the candidate. Ask, "In your experience with the candidate(s), did you feel that she or he brought the ability to work with you?"

    You are not looking for "approval to hire"; rather, you are looking for fit. Does the candidate have the capability of working well with the person or people involved?

14. *Consider debriefing as an opportunity to bring participants in the hiring process together to discuss the candidate(s) as a group.* For example, schedule a meeting with all participants to be held following the departure of the candidate. You, the hiring manager, are "convening an advisory board" to discuss the candidate(s). "What did you like best about the candidate(s)? What did you like least about the candidate?" Use a flip chart to capture the ideas.

15. *Make the hiring decision.* For example, consider the input from those involved in the hiring process—peers, problem-solving groups, and management representatives—and make your decision.

The hiring process at any company varies by position. However, an introduction of corporate culture into your hiring process at any level exposes the candidate to the inner workings of the work group *prior* to commencing employment. While this approach requires an increased investment of time and personnel, the savings that result from hiring only those employees that fit far outweigh the expenses.

HOW TO DEVELOP AND MAINTAIN PARTNERING RELATIONSHIPS WITHIN ORGANIZATIONS

Cathleen Hutchison

Cathleen Smith Hutchison *is managing partner of Conifer Consulting Group (PO Box 1147, Cedar Crest, NM 87008, 505-281-4496), a full-service human resource consulting firm specializing in managing corporate change, including change components such as culture change and reengineering. She is a past officer of the National Society for Performance and Instruction at national and chapter levels and of the International Board of Standards for Training, Performance, and Instruction.*

Partnering is teamwork between teams to achieve a set of goals. The teams can be work teams, functions, or divisions within an organization. Partnerships can also occur between organizations. This guide will focus on teams within organizations and describe a four-phase process in any partnering process.

Partnerships can be between two or more teams. For any partnership to work, there must be at least one mutual goal that all partnering teams feel is valuable to achieve. In operation, there must also be some level of openness, respect, and shared risk and responsibility.

Partnering relationships are becoming increasingly common as organizations attempt to find ways to become more competitive, while limiting their investment in equipment, resources, research, and development, and the like. Organizations are looking for and finding ways for their work teams to partner to minimize these investments.

In any partnering process, their are four main phases: (1) goal identification, (2) goal processing, (3) action planning, and (4) goal and process management (see Figure 40.1).

Phase 1: Goal Identification

The first action that must be taken is to identify goals for each of the potential teams. What does each team want to achieve? How do they and will they measure the success of their own team and of the partnering relationship?

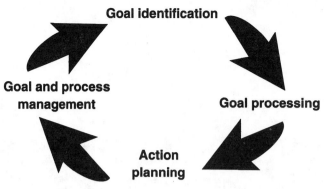

Figure 40.1.

Most teams already know what their mission and goals are. However, it may be useful to review them. Whatever issues have led the organization to explore a partnering relationship between these teams may also have affected the organization's goals and therefore the teams' goals. It may be appropriate to modify the organization's mission, vision, and/or goals at this time.

Likewise, it is an appropriate time to review how well the teams are operating internally. It is useful to explore process redesign, teamwork, skills assessment, resource and equipment needs, or other issues, as well as the partnering relationship, in order to maximize the organization's effectiveness and productivity.

Once each team has reviewed and modified its mission and goals, it will be useful to predict what goals the partners will have in common and where conflicts are likely to occur between them. What purposes do they share? What do both partners want to accomplish? The objective of this phase is to ensure that each potential partner has a clear understanding of what it is trying to achieve and is prepared to discuss its own positions and the current status of pertinent organizational operations.

A number of activities can be used to help teams to identify their goals. A menu of potential activities is provided in Table 40.1. Resources are available to provide more detailed information on how to conduct most of the activities listed. Some of the activities can be developed by the organization and/or the facilitator. Choose only those activities that are appropriate to the characteristics of the organizations and the environment within which they are operating.

Phase 2: Goal Processing

During this phase, teams looking into a partnership compare their respective missions and goals. When the goals of each team are compared with those of the other(s), there will be some goals in conflict with each other, some which support each other, and if there is a possibility of partnership, they will have at least one major goal in common. If there are no goals in common, then there is no basis for the partnering relationship. A different type of relationship may exist or be negotiated, but, by definition, it will not be a partnering relationship.

Table 40.1.

Activity	Purpose	Description
Mission statement review development	To ensure fit of the current team's mission statement with the environmental and business issues affecting the organization and to ensure clarity of understanding of the mission statement for all key players of the team and the potential partnership	Analyze the environmental and business issues. Compare to and analyze the organization's and team's mission statement; analyze the fit. Identify key players to the partnership. Identify and develop appropriate communication strategies.
Visioning	To create a vision of a better tomorrow for the team that could be achieved through the potential partnership	Develop vision for the team—the best it could be. Develop vision for the partnership—the best it could be.
Goal setting	To review existing team goals and to establish goals to be achieved by the potential partnership	Review current team goals. Analyze for current environmental fit. Determine goals to be achieved by the potential partnership.
Goal analysis	To analyze and prioritize the team's goals in light of the potential partnership	Analyze goals for potential fit with the partnership. Prioritize the team's goals (use categories of high, medium, low and can subdivide within as necessary).
SWOT analysis	To determine what strengths, weaknesses, opportunities, and threats (SWOT) the team brings to the potential partnership and what the potential partnership brings to the team in those categories	Identify team's strengths, weaknesses, opportunities, and threats. Analyze how the partnership will affect these. Analyze how the team's SWOTs will affect the potential partnership.

Table 40.1. *(continued)*

Activity	*Purpose*	*Description*
Partnership goal projection and categorization	To analyze the team's goals in light of the potential partnership and to project which of them are likely to be mutual, in conflict with, or supported by the potential partner(s)	Review the team's current goals. Use best guess to categorize these into mutual, conflicting, and supporting goals with the potential partner(s). Discuss the rationale for the predicted categorization.
Team building	To strengthen the internal interactions and interpersonal operations of the key players of the team	Build trust and working relationship within the group of identified key players of the team. Ensure shared perspectives on the team, the organization, and the potential partnership.
Self-assessment questionnaire	To determine readiness and appropriateness of partnering for the team	Analyze the team's readiness to take part in a partnership at this time. Analyze the appropriateness of the team entering into a partnership with the potential partner(s) at this time.
Team values audit	To assess the values guiding the internal interactions of the team and to what extent they are operating within the team	Collect data on the values operating in the team currently. Analyze the strength of the values. Analyze the appropriateness of the values to support and facilitate achievement of the goals.
Partnership parameters and requirements analysis	To determine the constraints within which a potential partnership would have to operate, to set the go–no go criteria for partnering	Identify the limits beyond which the team is unwilling to move in order to achieve the partnership.

The partnering teams identify which of their goals fall into the categories of mutual goals, conflicting goals, and supporting goals. Together, they analyze the goals that have been listed.

✓ Mutual goals are discussed to ensure that all aspects of each goal are truly mutual and to expose any underlying conflicts that may be included, but overlooked. (Unequal priorities for a mutual goal would be an example.)

✓ Conflicting goals and any identified conflicting areas of mutual goals are discussed to understand the sources, pressures for, and reasons behind the conflict. What are the differences in performance measurements—in reward and recognition systems? How do values and culture vary in the partnering teams? What are the relative priorities each team places on issues and expectations? What drives these various differences? Don't try to solve these conflicts right away. The first purpose is to truly understand them.

✓ Supporting goals are discussed to identify areas where support can be beneficially provided by one or more of the partners to achieve one or more of the other partners' goals. During the discussion, the partners also reach agreement on the parameters for what the support will include and how it will be delivered.

Discuss issues of openness and respect for each others' ability to contribute. How do the partnering teams currently share responsibility that involves them both? How can responsibility be shared more effectively? Analyze the potential risks for each party. Assess and agree on appropriate levels of risk and responsibility for each partner. Describe, discuss, and analyze each team's relative priorities. The purpose of this phase is to truly understand the perspective of the other potential partner(s) in the relationship.

A menu of potential activities for this phase is included in Table 40.2.

Phase 3: Action Planning

Now that the partners have identified their common goals and have both identified and reached an understanding of the areas of conflict, they are ready to move into planning what the partnership will look like. What will they do to achieve their common goals? How will they treat each other as they interact? How will they communicate with each other? How will they signal problems and difficulties as they arise? How will they address problems and difficulties? How will they remove or reduce the existing conflicts? What compromises can be made? What information will be shared? When? How? By whom? What values will guide their daily interactions with each other?

Table 40.2.

Activity	Purpose	Description
Goal comparison discussion	To discuss each other's goals and compare what each of the partners is trying to achieve	Identify the goals of each team. Compare the goals of each team. Analyze the fit of the goals of the partners.
Conflicting goal source and rationale exchange exercise (walk a mile in my shoes)	To share the sources and rationales for each team's perspective on a conflict between the partnering team and to reach understanding of those sources and rationales	Identify team goals in conflict with the partner's goals. Analyze the source and rationale for each goal for the team. Discuss each with the potential partner.
Supporting goal analysis	To analyze goals that are not mutual but the are not in conflict for opportunities for the partners to actively support the achievement of each goal	Identify goals that could potentially be supported by the partnering team. Brainstorm ways to support each other's goals.
Partner's goal reflection exercise	To reflect back to the other partner what one has heard and understood of its goals, issues, and constraints	Identify and discuss each team's goals, issues, and constraints. Summarize the other team's goals, issues, and constraints. Verify the accuracy of the summary.
Meta-perception exercise	To share feedback with partners about what it is like to work together from each perspective; to being to model openness	Identify issues and perceptions of the other teams (best with multiple partnering teams). Share the perceptions Identify actions to alter unwanted perceptions.

Table 40.2. *(continued)*

Activity	*Purpose*	*Description*
Partnering interview	To share feedback with partners about what it is like to work together from each perspective	Identify issues and perceptions of the other team. Share the perceptions Identify actions to alter unwanted perceptions.
Partnering assessment rating	To assess your partner's performance around specific kinds of behaviors and share that information with them	Identify values and behaviors needed to be operational in both teams to support and facilitate achievement of mutual goals. Develop assessment rating instrument on values. Complete on each other. Share and discuss assessment results with potential partner(s).
Partnership values audit and clarification exercise	To analyze the values needed for effective interpersonal interaction in the partnership and to assess to what extent the key players demonstrate these values and practices	Identify values and behaviors needed to be operational in both teams to support and facilitate achievement of mutual goals. Conduct audit of values in operation and extent to which they exist in each team and specifically in key players. Share and discuss results with potential partner(s).
Commitment analysis	To assess the level of commitment each partner brings to the partnership and to determine ways to increase the level of demonstrated commitment	Identify behaviors that demonstrate commitment to the partnership. Develop instrument to assess level of demonstration of behaviors. Share and analyze results. Create action plan to increase demonstration of commitment.

Table 40.2. *(continued)*

Activity	*Purpose*	*Description*
Priority assessment	To assess the priority that each of the partners places on individual goals, to compare these priorities, and to strategize ways for each to meet and support these priorities most effectively	Identify goals of each team. Prioritize importance to each team of achieving the goals identified by each team. Compare priorities. Discuss implications of the two (or more) sets of priorities.
Resource analysis	To determine the type and extent of the resources each of the partners has available for working the partnership issues and processes	Identify resources needed for achievement of partnership goals. Identify resources available from partnering teams. Compare availability of resources with required resources. Analyze gaps.
Trust analysis	To assess the levels of trust and areas of mistrust that exist between the partners and to determine actions that can be taken to increase the level of mutual trust	Identify areas of trust and mistrust between the potential partners. Analyze the extent and implications for the partnership of areas of mistrust. Identify actions that can be taken to increase trust.
Risk and responsibility analysis and clarification	To analyze the levels of risk and responsibility currently taken by each of the partners and determine equitable levels and ways of sharing risk and responsibility	Identify levels of risk and responsibility being taken currently by the potential partners. Identify levels needed for the partnership from each partner. Discuss gaps. Determine ways of bridging gaps.

Table 40.2. *(continued)*

Activity	Purpose	Description
Gap analysis matrix exercise	To assess the levels of openness, respect, and shared risk and responsibility that exist and what is needed for effective operation of the partnership and to determine the extent of the gap between those levels	Identify levels of openness, respect, and shared risk and responsibility being taken currently by the potential partners. Identify levels needed for the partnership from each partner. Discuss gaps. Determine ways of bridging gaps.
Partnership RAW test	To determine if entering into a partnership with this partner, around these goals, at this time is realistic, achievable, and worthwhile (RAW)	Identify goals of the partnership. Analyze the reality, achievability, and worth of attempting to enter into a partnership with these partners at this time.

When all relevant issues have been discussed, partnering agreements will be drawn up regarding not only what will be done, but also how people will interact. Early on in the relationship, until the teams become used to partnering with each other, it may be useful to have these agreements written down.

The purpose of this phase is to agree on what goals and actions are to be included in the partnering relationship and to also agree on how the partners will operate and work with each other to achieve these goals.

Table 40.3 lists a menu of potential activities for this phase of the partnering process.

Table 40.3.

Activity	Purpose	Description
Partnership statement	To describe, in writing, how the partners operate with each other	Define and agree on the way the partners will operate with each other during the partnership.
Action plans	To describe the actions to be taken in the partnership (by whom, by when) and what results are expected	Identify the actions to be taken in the partnership (include actions around resources, trust, commitment, openness, respect, shared risk and responsiblity and perceptions of each other, as well as goals of the partnership). Assign responsibilities and accountabilities. Identify targeted results and milestones.
Partnering agreements	To formally agree between the partners what will be done and how it will be done	Develop a formal agreement on action plans.
Partnering process reengineering	To create processes within and between the partner's teams that will most effectively achieve the mutual goals of the partners	Define processes as they should be to achieve mutual goals. Create joint implementation plan for new processes.
Communication plans	To develop communication strategies that will effectively address communication issues within and between the partners regarding partnership issues	Identify types of information to come from the partnership. Identify who needs to know each type of information. Identify the form information is needed in. Identify a method to share information that meets all identified needs.

Table 40.3. (continued)

Activity	Purpose	Description
Sunset clauses	To determine appropriate review dates and possible dissolution dates for aspects of the partnership and/or the partnership in general	Identify review milestones for for the partnership and aspects of the partnership.
Monitoring agreements	To determine and agree to methods of monitoring the the results, processes, and interpersonal interactions of the partnership over the run of the partnership	Identify when and how actions and accomplishments of the partnership should be monitored. Schedule monitoring milestones.
Decision-making guidelines	To determine guidelines key players will use for decision making—who decides, what issues, how to decide, and how to communicate decisions, etc.—for optimum effectiveness of the teams and the partnership	Identify potential problem areas in decision making. Identify guidelines for decision making. Communicate guidelines to all potential decision makers in the partnership.
Key player communication and buy-in	To communicate all relevant aspects and issues of the partnership to key players and to obtain their buy-in and commitment	Identify the different aspects and issues of the partnership. Identify who with each team (or beyond) requires input, should be advised, or needs to take an active part in each aspect and issue. Develop plan for sharing issues and gaining necessary input.

This is an ongoing part of the partnering process. Mutual goals, conflicting goals, and supporting goals must be continually monitored, managed, and discussed by the parties to the partnering relationship. New goals may arise in any of the categories as the partnering relationship grows and develops over time. Environments and constraints will change for one or both of the parties, and the relationship must keep pace with these changes. If these issues are not periodically reviewed and revised, the relationship will begin to deteriorate. Appropriate time frames and formal review points should be scheduled. Informal monitoring agreements should be designed to flag additional review points as they become necessary.

In addition to goals, the process that the teams use to interact with each other must also be monitored, managed, and discussed. Without ongoing openness, respect, and sharing of responsibility and risk, the partnership will begin to deteriorate every bit as much as if the goals change, if not more so.

The purpose of this phase is to keep the partnership effective, dynamic, and viable on an ongoing basis.

A menu of potential activities for this phase is provided in Table 40.4.

Table 40.4.

Activity	Purpose	Description
Partnering agreement status meetings	To review and assess progress and status on partnering agreements on a regular and ongoing basis	Analyze how well agreements are being met. Compare behaviors and accomplishments with agreed-on targets. Assess gaps. Determine actions needed.
Sunset clause review meetings	To review aspects of the partnership or the partnership as a whole in terms of the value of continuance	Analyze how well the partnership has achieved goals to date. Analyze evolving goals for the partnering organizations. Analyze value of continuing the partnership Identify parameters of partnership for the future. Identify new review milestones.
Milestone meetings	To review and assess the status of the partnership at predetermined milestones and time frames	Analyze how well targets and results are being achieved. Determine needed actions Identify new milestones and targets.
Key player values and practices audit	To determine the extent to which key players in the partnership demonstrate the values and practices identified as critical to the success of the partnership	Identify behaviors and values needed for achievement of the partnership. Survey constituents on the demonstrated behaviors of each key player. Share feedback with individual key players. Develop action plans. Repeat at appropriate milestones throughout the life of the partnership.

All four phases must be addressed in order to achieve effective partnering relationships. There are numerous methods to achieve the purposes of each phase. Some are more appropriate with one partnership, some with another. There is no one right prescription for a method to achieve successful partnering. The method should be tailored to meet the needs and characteristics of the partners.

REFERENCES

Hutchison, Cathleen Smith. 1991a. Partnering success stories. Unpublished concept paper. Conifer Consulting Group: Conifer, CO.

Hutchison, Cathleen Smith. 1991b. Partnering. Unpublished concept paper. Conifer Consulting Group: Conifer, CO.

All concept papers can be obtained from Conifer Consulting Group by calling 505-281-4496.

About the Editors

Mel Silberman, Ph.D., is President of Active Training (26 Linden Lane, Princeton, New Jersey 08540, 609-924-8157, mel@tigger.jvnc.net). He is also Professor of Psychological Studies in Education at Temple University where he specializes in instructional design and team building.

He is the author of:

> *Active Training* (Lexington Books, 1990)
> *101 Ways to Make Training Active* (Pfeiffer & Co., 1995)
> *Active Learning* (Allyn & Bacon, 1996)

He is the editor of:

> *20 Active Training Programs, Vol. I* (Pfeiffer & Co., 1992)
> *20 Active Training Programs, Vol. II* (Pfeiffer & Co., 1994)

Mel has consulted for hundreds of corporate, governmental, educational, and human service organizations worldwide. His recent clients include:

AT&T International
Merrill Lynch
Automated Data Processing
Bristol Myers-Squibb
American Insurance Group
Hoffman-LaRoche
Bell Atlantic
ARCO Chemical

Midlantic Bank
Texas Instruments
Meridian Bank
Franklin Quest
J. P. Morgan, Inc.
U.S. Army
Hospital of the University of PA
Penn State University

He is also a popular speaker at professional conferences.

Carol Auerbach is an independent management consultant (609 Kingston Rd., Baltimore, MD 21212, 410-377-9257). She is a graduate of Duke University and holds an M.Ed. in Psycho-educational Processes from Temple University. A former trainer for Mellon Bank and CIGNA Corporation, she now designs and conducts training on a wide variety of topics. This is her second experience assisting Dr. Silberman; she collaborated with Mel previously on *Active Training* (Lexington Books, 1990).